# Death and Life in
*Morazán*

# Death and Life in
# *Morazán*

## A PRIEST'S TESTIMONY FROM
## A WAR-ZONE IN EL SALVADOR

FATHER ROGELIO PONSEELE
talks to
MARÍA LÓPEZ VIGIL

**Catholic Institute for
International Relations**

First published 1989
Catholic Institute for International Relations (CIIR)
22 Coleman Fields, London N1 7AF

Originally published as *Muerte y Vida en Morazán* by UCA Editores,
Universidad Centroamericana José Simeón Cañas
San Salvador, El Salvador, Central America,
1987

**British Library Cataloguing in Publication Data**
Vigil, María López
    Death and life in Morazán.
    1. El Salvador. Catholic Church — Biographies
    I. Title  II. Muerte y vida in Morazán. *English*

    ISBN 1-85287-036 2

Translated by Dinah Livingstone
Edited by Mike Gatehouse
Cover and text design by Jan Brown

Printed in England by the Russell Press Ltd, Gamble St, Nottingham NG7 4ET

# Contents

# Introduction

Injustice, gross disparities of wealth and military domination make up the recent history of El Salvador. The terrible bloodshed, murder and mutilation of opponents of this injustice have made this tiny, overpopulated country a Christian symbol, what Jon Sobrino called 'a crucified people'. In El Salvador the church is at its limit, at the same time discovering itself on the boundary of immense human evil and losing itself in its chosen marriage with the poor, 'the crucified'.

The tension of this loss and discovery has uncoiled in different forms of action or has been transformed into a theology that carries this tension, sometimes reading like poetry. The context of this theology, the experience from which it has flowered, is unbearably alien to many Christians in the developed world, indeed for all those who did not live through the limit-situation of Nazism and the struggle against it. We have become accustomed to deal with it only as mediated through the prism of theological language.

But, as Bonhoeffer said, 'The first confession of the Christian community before the world is the deed which interprets itself.' It is to this 'deed' rather than 'theological word' that this book addresses itself. Nor is it a deed which the vast majority of us in the rich world will ever have contemplated choosing, let alone doing. This is a book about Father Rogelio Ponseele, a Belgian Catholic missionary priest, who chose as a Christian pastor to minister to Salvadoreans in the area of the country controlled by the FMLN guerrillas.

The book is the product of an extensive interview with María López Vigil translated from the Spanish with such skill that the reader will get to know Father Ponseele almost intimately in the

1

course of it. The text is entirely direct speech, an account of several years of this remarkable priest's life. In the original, Vigil wrote an introduction, describing Ponseele — 'tall, sturdy, fair-haired and red-faced. Father Tomato they sometimes call him' — and put him in the context of the history of the church and liberation struggles in Latin America.

The original introduction did not address the context in which the story would be interpreted outside El Salvador, the gulf between the experience of the Latin American church and the Christians of the developed world. But it is important to put Father Ponseele's story into this context to avoid it being misinterpreted.

It is not only the friends of the Church of the Poor who will interpret this singular and special 'confession', not only the liberation theologians who know well the choices and options open to Christians in this context, but also its opponents, who often know very little save their own narrow ideological ghetto. And in this ghetto the history of the church and liberation struggles is, at best, simply one of foolish clerics, wicked communist infiltrators, and gullible peasants.

For the enemies of the church today, the stereotype of the whisky priest has given way in Latin America to the guerrilla priest. He stares out from *Chick Publications*, pouring out of California into Latin America, a symbol of the Antichrist armed with an AK-47, waiting to invade the US embassy with his Marxist cronies. He is the basic figure used in the propaganda barrage against the Church of the Poor in Latin America, the alibi for persecution.

Firstly Father Ponseele's life with the people of Morazan and with the FMLN guerrillas is *one* of the choices open to Christians and priests. It is obviously a very unusual choice, numerically, for Catholic priests, even for those who have made an option for the poor, and it is this almost unique quality that makes the following pages so fascinating. The propaganda attempt to pretend that the Church of the Poor can be summed up, dismissed for the right or authenticated for the left, by the witness of such a ministry is nonsense. Such a ministry does not stand *for* the rest of Christian witness in the limit situation of El Salvador; it stands *with* the rest as part of a spectrum of Christian response to the crisis of the poor. The book reveals to what an extent it is, precisely, a special vocation.

Secondly the propaganda stereotype of the guerrilla priest is laid to rest by this book. Father Ponseele refuses to carry arms and

2

this refusal is understood and acknowledged in a variety of ways by the guerrillas. His motivations are in the deepest sense pastoral and flow not from some abstract ideological fixation, but from a practical concern for people and a faith commitment to the poor. His interest in Marxism seems absolutely minimal. He is carried by his faith to where the poor are — just like a priest choosing an inner-city ministry — and the poor happen to be with the guerrillas. And he suffers no less than the worker priest or the inner city priest the dilemmas of a changed sociological definition of his priesthood.

This book vividly recreates the warmth, vision and humanity of an exceptional man and an exceptional priest. His is a story of a Christian living out a discovery of the poor, a story of deeds, and so, in its special way, a confession of faith. CIIR hopes that its insights may not be without interest for the many whose choices occur in a context very different from death and life in Morazán.

**Ian Linden**
September 1989

# 1

# *Not a bad little priest*

Before the 'Football War' I didn't even know El Salvador existed. It was an unknown country for us in Belgium. The only thing I had heard about El Salvador in my whole life was to do with this 'Football War' with Honduras. Before that, no news at all. And after it, not another line... ever!

I had been a priest in Europe for five years, giving religious education lessons and looking after students in a school. That's all I did. Sometimes I think if I had stayed in Belgium I wouldn't have been a bad little priest, not so bad, but... And what if I'd stayed in San Salvador? I didn't stay, and by then it wasn't easy to do so anyway, because of the repression. I came here to a war-front. I feel happy here in Morazán, because I think I'm taking part in a process which is of critical importance for this people.

It was a very big step for me to leave Belgium and go to El Salvador. That was in 1970. It was the first time I had ever been out of Belgium and I was nervous. Where am I going, what am I going to do, will I be able to do it? I was afraid all right, no point in denying it. But we Flemings hide our feelings a lot, including fear. My farewell to my family was a cold affair. I remember we just shook hands, as if we had an agreement not to cry.

I knew nothing about El Salvador. What's more, I hardly spoke any Spanish. A few words, a little grammar, just enough to get started. I was terrified of looking ridiculous. I felt much too shy. Now I even think in Spanish, even pray in Spanish. I don't pray in Flemish any more. I always talk to God in Spanish. I do sometimes say the Our Father in my Flemish language. That's all that's stayed with me.

A lot of journalists come here to Morazán. They are interested in my job, the church's pastoral work. They think it's very odd to find a priest at a war-front. They come with their European ideas. And in Europe Marxism is atheistic, isn't it? They find it very peculiar that here is a Marxist-Leninist revolution going on with priests getting mixed up in it. I feel this in the questions they ask. Of course their interviews are a lot shorter than this one. Now I have talked a lot with you. Why, I have almost made my confession!

## Working class dignity

My home village is called Gullegem. It's about 90 miles from Brussels, near Bruges. I was born in 1939, at the beginning of the Second World War. I come from a working-class family, something all of us were proud of. This influenced my childhood. There were seven of us children in the family. The other strong influence on our lives was that my eldest brother was disabled and mentally retarded. He reached a mental age roughly that of a one-year-old, but he lived to be 34. For his entire life my parents had to look after him, feed him, put him to bed. He needed all the care and attention of a baby but for a body which grew to adult size, for his entire life, if you can call it a life. I always remember the love and dedication with which my parents looked after him. Such generosity. I think their Christian vision of life was reflected in that conscientious generosity. Wherever he was, at a meeting, at work, whatever the time, my father would drop everything and go home to carry my brother up to bed because he was very heavy and my mother couldn't lift him. Our parents' tremendous generosity to our brother left an indelible impression on all us other children.

My father — his name was Marcel — worked in linen weaving. I always remember him as the secretary of a Christian organisation of bread and coal co-operatives. He was also involved in educational organisations, and he was the village mayor. He could only do multiplication and division — I think he only reached third or fourth grade in school. In those days you didn't need many qualifications to be a mayor, you just had to be a good sort. Nowadays in Belgium you have to have a university degree to reach a position like that. My father wanted to study, to know more. I remember that when we came home from school with those terrible maths problems no-one can do, my father sent us

6

to bed and stayed up half the night trying to solve them. I remember him with great admiration. He was secretary of the bread co-operative and he never brought home a penny from the funds. On the contrary, he dipped into his own pocket for the good of the co-operative, and the bread at our table was almost always stale.

'If there is stale bread left over, where else can I take it but home?' he used to say.

He was the secretary and he could have brought us the best bread in the bakery, but he always brought us the leftovers. So we got used to eating stale bread. And it was strictly forbidden to go and get fresh bread from somewhere else because we had to eat the co-op bread! We didn't protest; we agreed with him. The success of the co-op, being workers and eating stale bread were all part of the same thing. We were proud of it in our family. As children, this was our contribution, not to complain at table, because our father was doing important work and we were proud of him.

My father was a much loved mayor. Even though he was a worker and had been elected by the workers' organisation, the middle-class people liked him. The socialists liked him too. On May Day the socialists held a rally in the village, with a festival. There were only a few socialists but all good people. They sang the *Internationale*, I remember, the same song that I sing here now at the front (who would have thought it then!)... Catholics did not go to the rally. One year, as my father watched them march past from a distance his face turned sad:

'What good people they are, what a pity they have turned away from God.'

A major influence at that time on the village and our household was Joseph Cardijn, the founder of the JOC, the Young Christian Workers. This priest stimulated the workers' movement. He was a visionary, and brought new energy. I went to hear him several times. Thousands and thousands of young workers would gather to hear him. When he arrived they clapped louder and louder, and shouted: 'Cardijn, Cardijn, Cardijn!' I couldn't stand all that fervour. By then I had already noticed that Cardijn never really said anything, but just kept repeating the same thing over and over:

'Young workers, we are children of God and we have dignity!'

As he said it he thumped his chest and the thumping sound could be heard over the loudspeakers.

'We are workers, we have dignity, we are children of God, brothers and sisters of Jesus!'

That was his whole message. That is, he said other things too, but his constant theme was the dignity of the worker. My pride in being a worker and my sense of the dignity of workers comes from those days and from my family. That's why when I arrived in El Salvador, I was upset to find in Zacamil that Salvadoreans didn't like to admit that they were workers.

'What do you do, where do you work?'

'I'm a student.'

And I knew this meant he worked in a factory and studied at night. The peasants weren't like this. You could see they were proud of being peasants. I think Christian faith has never given Salvadorean workers any pride in being workers. But it has given them pride in being a people. And pride in being a poor people. Isn't that the same thing?

We were poor but I never went hungry. My mother — Yvonne, she was called — knew all about poverty. She was the oldest girl in a family of 14 children. My grandmother had died very young and my mother had to be a mother to this large family and keep order in the house. It was very hard for her. This is why she was so strict, stricter than my father. To get anything we had to go to my father, because my mother laid down the law and made sure it was obeyed: home at a certain time, in bed at a certain time. That's the way it was. We had to go to Sunday mass at 6 a.m. because she said the later ones were for idle good-for-nothings. If we had been out having fun on Saturday night, we wanted to sleep longer, but this was out of the question. And never mind whether we had a headache or something else, we always had to go to mass at this time. She was very strict and very aware of poor people's problems. She used to tell us how one of her brothers went to the dentist to have a tooth out. And the dentist asked:

'Right my lad, do you want it with or without pain?'

And my brother was terrified.

'Show me how much money you've got on you.'

The boy showed him his few small coins.

'Well you'll just have to put up with the pain.'

He did not have enough to pay for the anaesthetic. So he had to have his tooth out in agony. I heard her tell this story many times.

She always taught us to have great respect for the old and the humble. Children have a bad habit of laughing at people with

8

handicaps and old people. This was a terrible thing to do in my house, a major crime! Bad enough to earn you a beating and being sent to bed without our 'little cross'. It was the custom in my home for our parents to make a little cross on our foreheads before we went to bed. Going to bed without it was enough to make us cry for hours on end. Not giving us the little cross meant total rejection, it was the biggest thing they could refuse us.

My mother was very Christian, very Catholic, but a bit anti-clerical. She told me several times about something that had annoyed her so much that she never forgot it. A priest came to her house. As they were a poor family there were not enough chairs for everybody, the chairs were always in use and warm, from the heat of people's bottoms. One day when the priest came, they moved one of the children from a chair to offer it to the priest. He refused it, annoyed because it was warm. My mother told this story with such hatred...

She always criticised the clergy for being idle layabouts. And when I told her I wanted to be a priest, she warned me:

'Make sure you don't just loaf about!'

She had a brother who became bishop of Ubangi in the Belgian Congo, but she didn't get on well with him. When we went to one of his services she couldn't stop laughing, because as a bishop, during mass, he had to keep taking off and putting on his little red skull-cap. And this tickled her a lot. She made fun of it. Later, when he retired, this uncle said to me:

'I am still prepared to do a lot for the Belgian missionaries in the Congo, but not for the blacks, nothing for them!'

I was really shocked. We couldn't understand how a missionary who had been working with black people for 30 years could hate them so much. He couldn't stand them. It's as though I had spent 30 years in El Salvador and hated Salvadoreans...


**The devil you know**
My family were very Catholic but not over-pious. We went to mass on Sundays, said our prayers at bed-time. We criticised priests and at the same time we respected them. My vocation to be a priest came from my family and the social concern it taught me. Perhaps I also had a personal inclination to prayer and religion. I always wanted to do something for the poor. It was a vague idea but one which always stayed with me. At 14 I finished

9

primary school and went on to high school to learn to be a teacher. I thought I could be a teacher. I liked the idea of it.

The high school was run by priests, and seemed almost like a seminary. I remember I was very devout. There were two masses on Sundays, mass every day, vespers and devotions in honour of the Blessed Sacrament... For a lot of the students this was all a bit much, but it didn't bother me. I liked being in chapel on Sundays, I liked mass, I loved singing. But the idea of becoming a priest hadn't even occurred to me. I was very rebellious. I contradicted everything the priests said and did things I wasn't supposed to do. My friends from that time have said to me:

'We never understood how you got into the seminary because you were a terror at school, always tormenting the teachers.'

I have never liked smoking but I did it then just because it was forbidden. When I finished high school at 19, I don't know why, but I got the idea of going into a seminary and becoming a priest. It was as much of a surprise to me as it was to everyone else, this idea. With my rebelliousness, I was the last person anyone would have thought of.

I think I stuck the seminary because I was so pig-headed. It was a terrible discipline and I tried to keep my spirits up by getting out of some things. The teachers used to say to me:

'If you're neglecting so many of your duties, perhaps you should consider whether this is the right place for you.'

There were a good many things I neglected, but I liked seminary life because it was communal. By God it was hard, though. We had to go to confession every week. And what sins can you commit in a seminary? It was a real cross for me, having to confess every week, but you had to go; they always checked up on you. I always accused myself of the same things. Lack of attention to the readings, that sort of thing, trivial stuff really... Our failings never change, do they? The spiritual director said to me one day:

'All right, if you can't cope with the spiritual reading, you should ask yourself seriously if you are going to stay on here.'

They gave me several warnings. But I stayed on.

I spent six years in the seminary, two years studying philosophy and four theology. In my second year of theology I had to do my military service. We studied in the morning and in the afternoon we did military training. They taught us exercises, running, and trained us as health auxiliaries. In that at least I learned something. They taught us how to handle weapons but as it didn't interest me in the slightest, I didn't pay attention. I didn't even learn to shoot! If I had known what sort of life I would be living now I would have paid a bit more attention. I remember very well one afternoon when we had target practice. I came last because I was such a bad shot. Others took good enough aim to score a few points, but weapons never interested me and I never got good marks as a soldier.

Everything was very orderly in the seminary, with rules for everything. Before you could become a priest there were the minor orders. We had to pass canonical exams, as they were called, in each of these. When we were doing one of these minor orders the director of the seminary summoned me:

'Which of the ordination texts made the most impression on you?'

'Well, actually none of them impressed me at all.'

He was annoyed and sent me to my room with orders to study the texts in depth until they made some impression on me.

At times like that I wondered what I was doing in the seminary, but in the end I always decided to stay on. I often went through various crises like this, but never really major ones. I am not into major crises! Little shocks, yes, and plenty of them. It was hard, but I went on out of sheer stubbornness. When it came to the canonical exam for the minor order of exorcist, who has power over devils, I got a teacher with a sense of humour, who was not afraid to criticise and make fun of all these exams:

'Rogelio, if you had the necessary instruments, do you think you would have the courage to cast out a devil?'

'Give me the instruments and I'll cast it out!'

'Okay, you've passed the canonical exam.'

It was that easy. Do I believe in the devil? No, what I believe in is evil. The devil is a personification of evil. And I am more and more convinced that evil exists. A person like Ronald Reagan is evil, don't you think?

I was ordained priest. I was twenty-six years old. For me the priesthood should always be linked to service, not to religious but to social service. I wanted to be a priest to accompany people who needed to become more aware, or to resolve their material problems. But they put me in a school to give religious education to children. I didn't think this was the right job for me. But I was very immature when I came out of the seminary and I made do with the school because I didn't think I would be strong enough to look after a parish properly and work with adults. These things happen in Europe... Very immature, wasn't it? These closed

11

seminaries... I spent five years in that school teaching and supervising the students. It was a frustrating task because you had to be on top of them, and behave like a policeman. There are priests who positively revel in work like that, so much the worse for them. I managed to get on well with the students, but I found it so boring...

I think another reason I decided to come to Latin America was for the adventure. I came looking for the unknown. That was part of the reason, in fact a lot of it. I always remembered what a fellow priest once said on a retreat:

'We are so passive, for heaven's sake. What's the matter with us, gentlemen? We are so passive, so passive. Let's do something even if it's something silly, let's just do something!'

I never forgot this. It's better to do something silly than to do nothing at all. Better to put your foot in it than not to take a step. Maybe I've done a lot of silly things in my life, but I think I have done something. It's better to make mistakes than do nothing. All this made me think.

While we were still in the seminary we received a letter from our bishop, Mgr De Smedt, Bishop of Bruges, addressed to all the priests and seminarians in his diocese. This letter made a great difference to my life.

He was attending the Second Vatican Council. In Rome he had met many Latin American bishops, who made him turn his attention to the church in Latin America. He said that a bishop is not just a bishop of his own diocese but of the whole church. And for that reason he was writing to us to suggest that we should consider going to work in Latin America. Just like that, in general terms, but with no details. The whole of Latin America. He told us it was a Catholic continent suffering tremendous poverty, and above all, with very few priests.

That was when we seminarians began discussing Latin America among ourselves. But it was still like a dream, something you think about but which will never happen. It didn't turn out like that. Not long afterwards some actually went: John, Stephen... they were off to El Salvador. Why to this country in particular, when we knew so little about it? I don't know.

I had a friend, Pedro. We were students together, we were together in the seminary, and were appointed together to teach religion and supervise in that school. One day he decided to go out to El Salvador. A year later I sent a note to my bishop telling him I wanted to go and join Pedro in his pastoral work. The bishop said I couldn't go yet because I was 'one of the best tutors in the whole of Europe'. According to him I was doing a tremendously good job and was irreplaceable, so I would have to wait. And I was fool enough to think I was really important! So I stayed in Belgium. In retrospect, I can see that the bishop wanted to test me, to see if my request was genuine and properly thought out. After a year they let me go. Perhaps part of it was my thirst for adventure. Yes, I think it was. I like adventure.

## Zacamil

I left Belgium in 1970. I had been a priest in Europe for five years. I knew nothing about Latin America, I knew nothing about anything. I was an immature and extremely timid person. From Belgium to Panama, fifteen days by sea. In Panama I spent a month in the parish of San Miguelito, where they were working with the 'God's Family' method. It was a method of pastoral work I was unfamiliar with. I enjoyed the experience. Part of the work was consciousness-raising. We were trying to build up the church by forming base groups conscious of what their Christian commitment really meant. Various US priests were working in the area with this method. And pastoral workers came there from all over Central America to learn it.

I arrived in El Salvador on 6 April and went to Zacamil, a district of multi-occupied dwellings on the outskirts of the capital, which is where the bishop had sent Pedro and me. But we did not confine ourselves to Zacamil. We also began working in other districts on the outskirts of San Salvador. Pedro said to me:

'Rogelio, we've got to start work. Let's go and see.'

The first thing was to visit people at home. House by house. People were surprised by these visits. They weren't used to the priest going from door to door. They were used to priests sitting in the parish office noting down masses and baptisms.

It was a terrible ordeal for me. I could hardly speak Spanish. I could only ask a few simple questions, which I had written down and prepared well in advance.

'How do you do? How are you? Where do you work? Where do you come from?'

As people came to Zacamil from all parts of the country I thought these were good questions to strike up a conversation. The difficulty was the replies: sometimes I didn't understand anything at all but I just said yes, yes to everything... Pedro told me I had to make these visits on my own. He was more of a talker and if I went with him he would do all the talking and I would sit like a wallflower in a corner, not opening my mouth. I had to learn to do without his support and not mind making a fool of myself. So I began going alone. It was really hard for me.

The language was a very serious problem for me. I found it very hard to learn, very hard indeed. I think this was because of my shyness, especially compared with Pedro. He just waded in and began talking, and wasn't worried about making mistakes. Not like me. I've always been shy, although I try to overcome it by cracking jokes. You know what else I did to overcome it? I played the trumpet. I had learned to play it at primary school. The trumpet has helped me in life to overcome my shyness. As a student I played in public, and although it terrified me, I gradually lost my fear. And at this time I used to play the trumpet when I went round the communities. Pedro and I went together, he put on a clown act and I played the trumpet. This was my salvation. I think that was why I had so much trouble learning the language. You have to make mistakes, you have to jump in at the deep end and swim...

As I learned the language, I began to learn about the situation in the country at the same time. People spoke to me about many things: the 1932 massacre, the things that had happened in the time of President Lemus, and of various other presidents. It was all new to me, so in this way I began to learn the history of El Salvador. Also I made myself read the papers from cover to cover. Even if it was all lies, there is always a grain of truth behind every lie, isn't there? I learned a lot this way. Every morning I spent an hour and a half reading and noting down all the words I didn't know and looking them up in the dictionary. We priests are also helped by the fact that we have to speak in public. At mass or a meeting we have to speak. I remember the first meetings with the communities we were forming. I put the questions I had prepared. Sometimes I didn't understand a single word of the replies, and I was supposed to draw out the conclusions from a whole discussion which I had not understood. People who talked in such a roundabout way, old people with no teeth... Really, I didn't understand a thing!

It was a year before I began to feel sure of myself and able to speak more or less adequately. In spite of this the people never humiliated me. They always encouraged me:

'But Rogelio, you speak better than us.'

Now I know the Salvadoreans better and I know that when they give so much encouragement it's because someone is doing something badly. I could hardly speak at all and they told me I was doing fine. Now I understand their psychology. When eventually they began to tease me, I was glad. It was a sign of confidence. I remember a meeting where the young people were mucking about. I arrived and shouted:

'What's going on here? This is sheer bedlam!'

But I said the word 'bedlam' (*relajo*) wrong. We have problems with the strong 'r'. This sound doesn't exist in Flemish. They laughed at me, mimicking my *'relajo'*. I was pleased because it was a sign that I was speaking better, which is why they dared to make fun of me.

The Salvadorean people are very warm. They have given me so much love and affection, although I'm a foreigner. I think for them Belgium must seem like some paradise with an abundance of everything. And they are very grateful that someone has been willing to come all this way to share with them. I felt very welcome from the beginning. It was this warmth that helped me learn the language and overcome my shyness.

The Salvadoreans are so different from the Belgians. Whenever I've gone back to Belgium I always want to return to El Salvador straight away. The people there are more open, more spontaneous, more friendly. The world looks completely different. The same thing strikes me whenever I go back. I'm in a queue for a train from Brussels to my village. It's cold, everyone is covered up, nobody looks at anyone else, or talks to anyone, they just wait in silence. Then I get on the train and sit opposite someone. I feel like starting up a conversation:

'How are you? Where do you come from?'

But you can't do it, it scares people off. Sometimes you manage to chat a little, but it's difficult. The train moves on and there I am sitting opposite someone for an hour, a hour and a half, two hours, without being able to say anything, or with the newspaper open to separate us. What a difference, eh? You never get that kind of solitary confinement in El Salvador.

When we arrived at Zacamil we found ourselves with a problem which for me was a blessing in disguise: there was no chapel. It didn't bother us much and we met in people's houses to celebrate mass. The work we began was simple. We followed the San Miguelito method. After making home visits and getting to know people well and making friends, we invited those who wanted to do so to form a Christian group. We met with these groups once a week and took each of them through a short course of ten talks. Each of the little groups consisted of from ten to fifteen people. At the end of the ten talks we invited them to go on to something else, a conference. First, though, we did the house-to-house visits and it was only after a year or so that we set up the short courses and the conferences. We always spoke about what was going on in the country and in their lives and in the lives of the people in the bible, all together. We had considerable success with this method, and got a lot of people to the meetings.

In Zacamil at the beginning we did not have that much success, because although it's a poor area, the people have at least some comforts, their home, a regular wage, however small, and so on. They have lots of problems as well, but the idea of 'getting on' has already got to them. And this makes it difficult for their consciousness to grow.

The shanty-towns: I was appalled. We began to make contacts in the shanty-towns as well, where people live piled on top of one another in cardboard and tin shacks, in ravines and gullies through which the sewers flow. They made a very strong impression on me. I had never seen poverty like this, the wretchedness of the people of these settlements seemed so awful. We went there too to make home visits. It was an area of drunks and prostitutes... At first people didn't trust us. This was because they were afraid that we were just looking in for a few days. Students who were doing research used to come sometimes, or people from some government scheme or other, but they too only stayed for a few days, because neither the project nor the people really interested them. At election time politicians would turn up too. But these people had never seen anyone who was prepared to come and keep on coming and stay on to help and listen to them. When they saw that we kept on coming, they began to see us in a different light. We turned up in these slums, we worked with the people, we were reliable. Thus we were able to form quite a number of study groups in these very poor areas.

There were things that really shocked me about the way people behaved. We would be having a meeting, or perhaps a mass. Someone would arrive late and immediately they would become the centre of attention. You could be preaching, concentrating so as not to lose your thread, but no chance... A late-comer would walk in, there would be greetings and calls to come and sit at the front, to find them a chair from over there, etc. Amidst all the confusion I was left high and dry. Later I realised that there was a lot of sense in what they did. Paying attention to the person arriving late was much more important than listening to what I was saying. That someone feels welcome at a meeting and can see that they are valued is far more important than what the priest says in his sermon. It used to shock me, though, and sometimes it still does. But they are right.

I was shocked, too, at the way children behave. They are allowed to do what they like. It's not that I don't like children but... Sometimes for a more solemn occasion, we would prepare everything for the service very carefully: so-and-so to read this passage, someone else to read that, then the procession... But the children would turn up and spoil everything! Sometimes they pulled off the altar cloth and started playing with it and no one told them off. The same thing happens here at the war-front. Children! And if the priest dares to tell them off people take a very dim view of it. I have learned my lesson now and I never do it.

I remember once we were celebrating Holy Week in Zacamil. After the way of the cross we arrived at the meeting-room, which was tiny. I had set out some chairs. When I got there I saw that the children had gone on ahead and were already occupying all the chairs. So I got angry:

'All children go outside please! The chairs are for the adults!'

But not a single adult was willing to sit down. And afterwards I was severely criticised for the way I had behaved to the children. The children didn't deserve that, because it was perfectly all right for them to spoil my plans if they wanted to, that was their right...

Obviously, I was not brought up that way. A great deal of discipline was expected from me. But I realise that if we invite families to take part, we have to accept their children's unruliness. How are we going to keep them quiet listening to something they don't understand? The Salvadoreans have taught me that it's more important to respect a child than to keep order.

### Violence

In our team of three priests, all of us Belgians, there were also some girls, sort of nuns, but not ordinary nuns, something else, something special. What happened with them was wonderful.

There were three of them, Salvadoreans. They arrived from the country, peasant girls come to prepare to become nuns in a famous congregation in San Salvador. Pedro used to challenge the sisters in this congregation constantly, trying to open their eyes and make them see the real poverty around us, and get involved, commit themselves. He was always criticising the peace and calm of the convent, and saying how comfortable it was to be praying and doing little or nothing to change things... Imagine it! After conversations like this the nuns ended up furious with him!

Little by little the sisters in this congregation, like many other people in Archbishop Romero's time, began to change and get involved. Three who really changed were the Salvadorean girls working with us. A strong feeling was growing up between them and they began to live in their own little community. They were the ones who knew best how to work in the shanty towns in those early days. They performed miracles. The men there were so macho, with such macho customs and yet they managed to work with them. They were deeply respected. If someone tried to get fresh with one of them, there was always someone else around who said:

'That's enough! These women must be respected.'

They were so young and they managed to do such excellent work in the slums. Silvia is dead now. In the general offensive of January 1981 she joined the Santa Ana front and they killed her in the massacre at Cutumay Camones. She is one of our community's martyrs. She gave her life with great generosity. My goodness, though, to reach that stage of commitment, how much we all had to change, both they and us!

Violence: what a change we had to make to our ideas on that subject. How did we begin to understand the problem of violence in El Salvador? It was very hard for us to understand. We had our set ways of thinking. During the early years in the Christian communities and the groups we were forming, in the initial meetings, we always used to listen to a recording of Martin Luther King's 'I have a dream' speech. Looking back it seems ridiculous that there we were listening to words in English which we barely understood. We had to follow them with a written translation in our hands. We admired Martin Luther King. I still do.

Non-violence! We were always keen supporters of non-violence. We spent years and years preaching it. We kept it up to the last moment, till the time of General Romero in 1978. Our ideal, which we presented as the Christian ideal, was non-violence. And we offered Martin Luther King as the embodiment of this method. The women were the ones who were most against violence, their minds were very closed against it. In every talk, it was non-violence and more non-violence. Of course more and more this preaching ran counter to the whole reality of the situation at that time. While the women were still speaking of non-violence they were sheltering (comrades) who had by that time joined underground organisations and went around armed. That's typical of the Salvadoreans: face to face with real people and events they are much more flexible than in a theoretical discussion. In theoretical matters they are as stubborn as can be, and will cling on to a whole series of preconceptions, but person to person they are flexible.

By now, as far as non-violence was concerned, all the doors had been slammed in the faces of a people desperate for change. Everywhere popular organisations started forming, and these were also armed organisations. We couldn't ignore this fact. Many of our Christians were 'organised' — belonged to the organisations. However, I have to admit that at the beginning, because of the need for non-violence, I did not accept this reality. I even went so far as to say at a meeting once that if any members of these popular organisations interfered in the community I would drive them out with a whip, like Christ driving out the money changers from the temple! I was really angry as I said it. That's how I felt.

Everything was changing, and this non-violence of ours, what did it mean? What was the point of it? What did it solve? This blind opposition to armed struggle was distancing us from the people. We were raising the consciousness of our people, and as a result many were joining the organisations and getting killed in demonstrations. They were taking up arms to defend themselves and organising in armed groups... And we, who had brought them thus far, kept going on about non-violence. We were moving away from the people or they were moving away from us.

I often think of Marbel, a girl of fifteen. She was highly intelligent. I often chatted to her in those last months of her life. She was a Christian and she was 'organised'. She had many discussions with her *compañeros*, her comrades, about God.

'No, I don't believe in God any more,' they used to tell her.

And she defended herself:

'Well, you believe in love, don't you? You've got a girlfriend, haven't you? So you believe in love?'

And of course they said they believed in it.

'Well, have you ever seen love?'

You see, the compas, the comrades, always came out with the fact that no one had ever seen God.

19

'God is love: you can't see love, it's something you experience.'

This is what she told them, very firmly. That's a theology, isn't it? She was such a lovely girl. She gave talks to adults on the political situation.

Her organisation decided to raid a bank. At that time this was how they got money to finance revolutionary activity. She was chosen to be in the group to do the raid. She told me she was going to do it a few days before. She was afraid, she said, but never mind.

They were all killed, Marbel too.

This helped me along the road to understanding violence. It was a time of demonstrations and activities like this. Protesting, demanding your rights, meant risking death. There would be a demonstration and when they came back to the community:

'How was it?'

'Okay, only three dead.'

'Not so many.'

And I didn't know any of the three. But one day they told me:

'They killed all six of them. Marbel as well...'

Marbel! That was why, because you knew those who were getting killed, you started to ask yourself questions about your own place in the struggle. That was how I began to understand.

I had to go and look for Marbel with her mother, going from one undertaker's to the next. She was so young and so good. When I think of her I refuse to believe there is nothing beyond death.

Silvia is dead too. They killed her as well. What a lot of fights I had with Silvia about this non-violence business. In the end I too was questioning our ideas of non-violence. If every avenue had been closed off to the people and the people were right, we ought not to be trying to impose our ideas on the people, but accompanying them on their road. We had to become more open, we had to reflect... That's how I was talking, and it annoyed me that a bunch of stubborn girls kept contradicting me. Especially Silvia. She stood up in a meeting, bible in hand, and told me my opinion was worthless. She kept knocking down all my ideas with quotations from the bible. Whereas I was suggesting questions for discussion. I insisted that we were doing the people a disservice with all our scruples about violence. That way the people would never dare organise, and it would hold back the struggle... But she didn't want to know, and just kept challenging me with her bible texts! I was annoyed, speechless.

We came out of all the meetings arguing and arrived at their house and carried on the argument on the steps and at the door... We were arguing as we went in, and still arguing when we came out. It was the year 1977 and we were still hesitant about all this. Many Christians from our communities were already organised and working underground. It was the people who made us understand, not the other way round. We raised the people's consciousness so far, to a certain point. From there on it was they, the people, who raised our consciousness.

I had a good teacher in those early days. Odilón. He sold puddings to earn his living. Not just to earn his living but to have enough free time to dedicate his life to the struggle. We became great friends. He was in his early thirties with a family and two or three children. He was a leader of our Christian community in Zacamil. He spent the night making puddings and went out first thing in the morning to sell them. He had his regular customers and didn't need to look for other outlets. He knew that he could sell so many in the university and another lot somewhere else. He ran from place to place, making more and more puddings. By 9 or 10 o'clock in the morning they had run out. His work was finished and from then on he was free to do other things: work for the organisation and work for the Christian community.

Odilón was a very good example for me. Some people used to say:

'We're in the organisation, so we can't do this or that any more because we haven't got time.'

When they said that I always thought about Odilón, how he managed to organise his life to earn enough to pay for his family's needs and still be active in other things. He was a great friend. He would arrive at the house with a pudding. It was delicious, and while we were eating it we would talk about the situation.

He insisted on the need for change. He tried to keep me well informed and he wanted to get me to move forward a bit. He was teaching me, winning me over. I got used to his visits. I used to say to the others:

'Here comes Odilón. We're going to eat pudding and talk about coffee!'

Sure enough. Odilón arrived, sat down, took out his puddings and offered them round. Then I would say:

'How are you, Odilón? What's going on?'

'The first thing we must understand is what is happening with the coffee...'

21

He always began in the same way, with the economic infrastructure, as he called it! Odilón, what a good friend he was! He was a teacher to me. Since I met him I have maintained that true revolutionaries are not those who do something by stopping doing something else, but those who spread themselves so they can do everything. Odilón also fell at Cutumay Camones in January 1981 during the general offensive.

## Monseñor

Ten years we worked in the suburbs of San Salvador, from 1970 to 1980. It was a long process for the communities and for us. As we got deeper into the work of raising people's consciousness, and as the people steadily organised themselves, more problems arose. In the church not a single bishop supported us. Along that road not a single one. Only Archbishop Romero and his auxiliary, Bishop Rivera. It was not just that the others didn't support us; they condemned us. The truth was we could only count on Archbishop Romero.

But before we could even count on him, there was a lot of ground to be covered, a whole process. Until he became Archbishop, Mgr Romero had been thoroughly reactionary. His appointment was a great disappointment to us. I met him when he was still an auxiliary bishop. At that time he was highly critical of the base communities. He hardly came near them, and when he did he was very negative. The truth was that we did not like Mgr Romero at all. At that time he appeared to be not just a conservative but even an evil man.

In our parish we had a fairly serious quarrel with him. It happened after an occupation of the National University, in 1972. A statement was issued by the bishops in which they came out clearly on the government's side, and justified its actions in terms of the dangers of subversion and communism. Our Christians were angry with the bishops, but as we felt we belonged to the church, we thought we should invite Mgr Romero to come and talk with us. He accepted, he arrived at the parish and we prepared a mass for him to concelebrate with three other priests. Everything went normally but after the gospel, he began to attack us in his sermon, accusing us of being political, of no longer being Christians. He rejected our commitment and offended the congregation. There was nothing nice about the way he did it. This was not an argument or a discussion, just an exchange of insults. People were deeply offended and argued back, bible in hand. It was a tremendous fight.

Pedro took off his alb and said the atmosphere was not right for celebrating the eucharist and we had better leave it because the whole thing had been a disaster. Perhaps we just didn't know how to carry on the discussion. *Monseñor* hadn't got a leg to stand on and fell back on his authority, insisting that he was right, because he was the bishop. He said this in an ugly tone of voice. We didn't finish the mass, everyone went home, and just a few went on discussing with *Monseñor*, who was in a rage. I remember that day I asked Bishop Romero:

'How can the church be so cut off from the poor, from the people?'

But he didn't answer. I think he despised us then. It was a really sad thing, that quarrel.

But after all it was a good thing that this happened. Years later when *Monseñor* had become Archbishop, he came back to the same place and the same people came to listen. I remember his first words: he said he remembered everything that had happened and he asked us to forgive him for what he had said that day. He asked our forgiveness! And he told us that he was determined to accompany his flock like a shepherd and that previously he hadn't understood what was going on. Such humility!

I can't think of another bishop who would do this. The change in *Monseñor* was a miracle. How did it happen? Well, I think in spite of everything he was always an honest man. He was prejudiced against us and we were prejudiced against him. Now we can see that he was never evil. We felt he was evil but that was our mistake, our prejudice. Deep down he was always honest, and surely anyone who is honest always arrives at the truth. He tried to do good as he understood it. And he was under many negative influences.

He was also always a man who prayed a lot, very religious. For him God was not an empty word. I think God is an empty word for some bishops. He's just their employer. For Archbishop Romero, even during his bad time, God was always Someone to whom he tried to respond as best he could.

He was a very religious man. When I think of him, I especially remember the day when the Popular Leagues occupied the church of the Rosary. The church was occupied, but masses and services continued. The compas checked everyone going in. A National

Guardsman tried to go in armed, as a provocation, and the compas took him prisoner. He wanted to start a fight inside the church and start shooting towards the street so that they could blame it on members of the League, or something like that. So they took him prisoner. Then *Monseñor* realised that the security forces were going to use this captured guardsman as a pretext and force their way into the church to rescue him, and there would be a massacre.

*Monseñor* decided to intervene. As I knew the League compas well, he asked me to go with him. We went to the church and while we were inside, the Guard started surrounding it. Negotiations began, the guerrillas released the guardsman, but things didn't end there, because the Guard remained outside, insisting they were going to enter the church. And the compas were at the door with their little pistols. We stood behind waiting to see what would happen. And *Monseñor* stood at the door trying to negotiate. The guards shouted at him 'You bastard!' This made a strong impression on him. Afterwards he said to me:

'That's the first time anybody has called me that.'

He was indignant, and also worried. He confessed to me afterwards that he was sure they were going to kill us all. There were some bad moments. And this is what I remember. It didn't occur to me to pray, but I saw him praying and the sight remains engraved on my memory. Pale, striding up and down and saying the rosary... This lasted one hour, two hours. He kept on saying his rosary. *Monseñor* told me afterwards that praying had been his only hope. What simple faith! This would never have occurred to me. But it did to him. He was a very religious man.

He was a shy man, but also a cheerful person. He told jokes and created an atmosphere of great warmth between himself and the people. This was a great thing for us Christians. It was also a great thing for us Europeans who are so used to there being an enormous distance between bishop and people. To get to see a bishop in Belgium you have to get past four or five doors, ask permission, ring up, make an application, wait a whole day... Not here. Here we saw something different: a bishop who lived with the people. So we got closer and closer to him then and this gave all the communities a tremendous feeling of really belonging to the church. In all the things that happened, happy or sad, in assassinations, massacres, in all their activities, we were there. And he was there with us. We valued *Monseñor* highly for his work, the efforts he made to meet everybody and to visit the most remote villages. From morning to night in his office, there were always people wanting to talk to him. He got close to the whole people. And the whole people came close to him. Not an easy thing for a bishop.

The last time I talked to him was in February 1980, a month before he was killed, when he went to Belgium to receive an honorary doctorate from the University of Louvain. I was in Belgium and I came back with him, carrying his suitcase for him.

The ceremony in Louvain was beautiful. It was a grand occasion in this prestigious medieval university with all the professors wearing their special ceremonial gowns. I knew *Monseñor* well enough to see that he was very nervous, because he was shy and he found it difficult to speak in front of all those academics. But he began by saying half a dozen words in Flemish, which won all their hearts. After five minutes he had lost his nervousness. He was a gifted speaker. From then on he might have been standing in his pulpit in San Salvador Cathedral, with all his usual gestures and eloquence. And what he said made a strong impact. There was tremendous applause. Before him some scientists spoke who were also being given doctorates. They were applauded politely, but *Monseñor* got an ovation. This is how he began his address:

I come from the smallest country in faraway Latin America. I come bringing in my heart, which is that of a Salvadorean Christian and pastor, greetings, gratitude and the joy of sharing the experiences of life.

I first of all greet with admiration this noble alma mater of Louvain. Never did I imagine the enormous honor of being thus linked with a European center of such academic and cultural prestige, a center where were born so many of the ideas which have contributed to the marvelous effort being made by church and society wonderful initiatives to adapt themselves to the new times in which we live.

Therefore I come also to express my thanks to the University of Louvain and, through it, to our sister church of Belgium. I want to think of this honorary doctorate as something other than an act of homage to me personally. The enormous disproportion of such a great weight being attributed to my few merits would overwhelm me. Let me rather interpret this generous distinction awarded by the university as an affectionate act of homage to the people of El Salvador and to their church, as an eloquent testimony of support for and solidarity with the sufferings of my people and for their noble struggle for liberation, and as a gesture of communion, and of sympathy, with the pastoral work of my archdiocese.

I could not refuse to accept the privilege of this act of homage if, by coming to receive it, I could come to thank the beloved church of Belgium for the invaluable pastoral help it has given to the church of El Salvador. It would not, indeed, have been possible to find a more suitable time and place time and place to say 'thank you' than this one, so courteously provided for me by the University of Louvain. So, from the depths of my heart, many thanks to you — brother bishops, priests, sisters and lay people — for so generously uniting your lives, your efforts, and your financial assistance with the concerns, the work, the exhaustion and even the persecutions experienced by our pastoral workers ['The Political Dimension of the Faith from the Perspective of the Option for the Poor', in Archbishop Oscar Romero, *Voice of the Voiceless*, New York, Orbis Books, and London, CIIR, 1985, p.177].

We came back together on the plane and talked quite a bit. He never mentioned the subject of death, he always spoke about life, and what had to be done. On that journey he talked a lot about his concern that the communities might turn into mere political organisations and nothing more, and that they would not retain their Christian identity and remain faithful to the church. He questioned me about this and asked me to tell him my own experiences. The other bishops were pressing him heavily on this point. I assured him that the work we were doing was pastoral, that the communities were continually engaged in bible study, and that if our people were organising in popular organisations, this was a consequence of their faith. He understood this very well but it was difficult for him because of all the accusations being levelled against him, saying that he was going about supporting political causes because priests like us, doing this sort of work, were really politicians, not priests. And the same went for the communities. He wanted arguments with which to defend himself. He asked me for some.

We talked about it at length, and also about his experiences during his stay in Belgium. He had been very impressed by the families of the Belgian priests and sisters working in El Salvador, which were large and very united. In El Salvador poverty, repression and war have broken up all the families. It's difficult to find a really close family. *Monseñor* found that very painful. On this journey he talked a lot about how to do pastoral work with families. He never switched off, he was always thinking about what to do.

I've noticed that as people move up in rank and responsibility, especially in the church, they became more reserved. More and more they're institution men. It's logical. They don't want to lose status. But with Archbishop Romero it was just the opposite. The great change in him took place when he reached the top. He lost his status and he lost his life. It's something unique in church history, a miracle.

*Monseñor* was a very passionate man. I'm profoundly grateful to him for his sense of what the church should be. Here at the war-front we try to be a bit like him — to accompany the people, and yet be always doing the work of the church.

## Repression

The repression opened our eyes. Repression against the people of the communities, when they made protests. And against priests. I lived through the killing of so many of our priests during those years. The first was Rutilio. And so many others. In January 1979 they murdered Octavio Ortiz, our *compañero*, my friend, who was a member of our pastoral team, who came from here, from Morazán... Rafael Palacios, Alfonso Navarro, Napoleón Alirio... I was at all their funerals. But their deaths never discouraged me. I think during those years Archbishop Romero was doing a great deal to encourage us. In these priests' funerals there was always a strong feeling of solidarity, which gave you a real lift. Church and people united, a church united with the people even to the point of shedding its blood, like theirs. Those deaths gave us courage. I felt pain and at the same time great encouragement to go on.

We were searched and raided time after time. Before they started killing priests, before 1977, there was a big raid. They had captured a boy and found the telephone number of our house on him. They forced him under torture to tell them that we had arms in the house. And they made him draw a diagram to show exactly where these arms were. They came to look for them. A great uproar in the house. Fortunately Pedro and I were there alone. The guards threw us face down on the ground, with their rifles, jabbed into our backs, while they searched. I was shaking all over, I wanted to run for it, run away and leave Pedro alone. I was very frightened.

There was a demonstration in San Salvador on 29 October 1979, after the junta took power. They killed more than thirty peasant demonstrators. They brought the corpses to the Church of the

Rosary and asked me to celebrate mass. Some priests strongly objected to my celebrating mass for people in the organisation. But that day I couldn't refuse. They were very poor people, peasants from these parts, from Morazán, who had gone to the capital to protest and demonstrate. And they had been killed. I'll never forget that mass with the thirty bodies round the altar in the sanctuary of the church, with the peasants and the families. The city people are colder, but the peasants know all the songs, readings, and prayers. They all join in. It gave me courage to watch these people, so deeply religious. I've never forgotten that mass, it made a deep impression on me. Those peasants taught me that resignation is not the same thing as conformism. For them death is part of life. I always speak about that mass when Europeans ask me:

'And what do you, as a priest, think about violence?'

I tell them that violence is not a theoretical problem but a practical problem, that you can only understand the violence of the people when you accompany the people. The problem of violence is the question of what side you are on, where you stand. I am struck by the fact that the bishops of Nicaragua don't condemn the violence of the contras. If anything, they support it... So the problem is not violence as such, but who is doing it and what for. The problem is what side we are on, from what viewpoint we look at life, who we are with, where we stand, when we take part? Don't you agree?

# 2

# *The Road to Morazán*

I never thought they would kill me. I just didn't believe it could happen to me. But then we had to start taking various security precautions, because we were all in danger and on the death squad lists. One measure we took was never to sleep at the house. During the day we worked as normal, but at night we went elsewhere to sleep. The worst was in 1980. After the assassination of Archbishop Romero, anything seemed possible. They're going to kill us all, we thought at the time. Or, maybe I wasn't so sure. Anyway, I never much liked security measures. By then Pedro had gone, and just Luis and I were left. One night I felt too tired to go out and look for somewhere to sleep.

'Luis, let's stay here tonight. There's no danger.'

'No, Rogelio. We've got to hide.'

That evening we left at about nine o'clock. At eleven the house was blown up by a bomb. It was completely destroyed. Both Luis and I would certainly have been killed if Luis had listened to me.

**OCTOBER 1980**

6 Security forces raid the home of a priest, Fr Manuel Antonio Reyes Mónico. He is dragged from the house and the following day he is found murdered.

Rural military patrols search the Archdiocesan Caritas warehouse at Aguilares.

A rural military patrol invades the sanctuary of the Aguilares church and fires into the air.

At 8 a.m., as he is leaving the Domus Mariae Mejicanos refuge, Francisco Antonio Castillo Hernández is seized by members of the security forces in plain clothes. Castillo, aged 22, a bricklayer from Mejicanos, was bundled into a taxi and taken to an unknown destination.

7 A powerful bomb explodes in the doorway of the Archdiocesan office in San Salvador at the San José de la Montaña Seminary.

10 Army personnel raid the priests' house in the parish of San Francisco, Mejicanos.

Army search raid on the refuge at the Domus Mariae retreat centre.

A combined security forces operation opens fire on the church at Aguilares. Troops enter the church, loot it and fire weapons inside the building.

Combined security forces raid on the parish house at Aguilares. Money and electrical appliances are stolen and much damage done.

The parish clinic at Aguilares is machine-gunned by combined security forces.

Combined security forces force their way into the Archdiocesan Caritas warehouse at Aguilares and steal clothing.

24 Fifteen powerful bombs are placed in the house of the Jesuit fathers in Colonia Jardines de Guadalupe in San Salvador.

27 A further explosion completes the destruction of the house of the Jesuit fathers in Colonia Jardines de Guadalupe in San Salvador.

Raid on the Domus Mariae refuge, Mejicanos. An attempt is made to destroy the only remaining serviceable parts of the transmitter of Radio YSAX, the radio station of the Archdiocese of San Salvador.

**NOVEMBER 1980**

5 The house of the Belgian priests who do pastoral work in the parish of Colonia Zacamil, San Salvador, is blown up. In the raid which followed minutes after the explosion, papers, photographs, cassettes, books, money and a duplicator are stolen. The uniformed security forces who carry out the raid and steal the property are the same people who planted the bomb.

7 Heavily armed men in plain clothes seize two youths who are students at the San José de la Montaña Seminary...

[A single page taken from *Persecution of the Church* a long report, covering just the year 1980, by the Legal Aid Office (Tutela Legal) of the San Salvador Archdiocese, San Salvador 1981.]

San Salvador was getting really dangerous. The repression was growing and we were all under threat. Time and time again they came to search the house. And we began to get threatening phone calls: that they were going to kill us because we were communist priests; that we must go; that they knew what we were up to. Threats. As things got more ugly, we had to take it seriously. The death squads were very efficient. We asked for shelter in a convent, and they gave us a little room where we could sleep — despite the fact that the sisters there were teaching the children of the wealthy. But in Archbishop Romero's time a lot of people opened up. After his assassination, things changed, and many people took a step back. Things in the Salvadorean church have changed an awful lot without Archbishop Romero.

One night there were two girls who also had a security problem and couldn't stay at home. As if it were the most natural thing in the world, we decided to take them to the convent where Luis and I were going. There was just the one little room with two beds and a mattress. There was just room for the four of us. We had the key to the convent, so without making any noise we crept in and made our way to the room...

By the time things became so difficult, we had already set up a great many communities. On Sundays we had mass after mass, all day long. At 6.30 in the morning I used to get into the car in Zacamil and off I went to one place after another. I had plenty of masses, but I didn't earn a penny. There are priests who will say seven masses in a day, just to earn cash. In all these communities the popular organisations had been growing rapidly. They were communities of the poor, and there is a point at which poverty and organisation go side by side, don't you think? As soon as they got organised, the Christians of our communities began to suffer repression. Many were killed. They were dragged out of their houses, killed, and their bodies just dumped nearby...

In the communities of Zacamil alone we had 600 killed, 600 martyrs. They were Christians and they gave their lives for their people. They are our martyrs... I have always insisted that we keep a record of all their names, so that we will remember them always. Someone is already doing that in San Salvador: their names, their dates, their circumstances and their lives. We can never let ourselves forget them. I've seen so many killed, and already I'm forgetting their names...

31

Nothing but problems here. The popular organisations have stepped up their activity a lot. And the repression has increased at the same rate. A member of one of our Christian groups was captured last Tuesday. He was a teacher. We don't know where he is or what has happened to him, but we haven't much hope of finding him alive. Bodies are found every day. Yesterday was the saddest day of my life. The missing teacher's pupils said they had seen his body on the outskirts of a village about an hour away from here. Together with his wife and some of his family, we went to look. The justice of the peace of the village had registered ten bodies the previous day. 'This is happening every day now,' he said. We thought that one of the ten, who had not been identified, might be our friend. But the body had already been buried. They gave us permission to exhume it, and we went to the cemetery with a pick and spade... We exhumed the body, which showed the marks of cruel torture, but it wasn't him... On our way back they came to tell us that they had found the body in the same place where we had been looking in the morning. We got there. There was a small group of people standing on a bridge. 'Every day bodies appear here,' they told us. 'This morning we buried a teacher.' But the details they gave didn't fit. While we were there, another body was found near the river, with the scars of torture. We turned it over, face upwards. But it wasn't him... Our friend's wife burst into tears. We will carry on looking for him, but I've no hope at all of finding him alive. God cannot be indifferent to so much suffering... (Extract from a letter dated 15 February 1980).

## Time for decision

Ever since the assassination of Father Octavio in January 1979, we had begun to consider leaving San Salvador. The atmosphere there was getting tenser by the day. By the end of 1980 I thought that that was it. In November that year — do you remember? — they had killed the leaders of the FDR, and a few days afterwards the US nuns... It was a difficult time. It was time to make decisions.

My goodness, it's a dangerous thing to do to take people by the hand and lead them, because they in turn will take the lead and take you further than you intended! By the end of 1980 the compas were preparing for the general offensive. The 'final offensive', they called it. There was no way we could stay in San Salvador. We would get killed.

I had two alternatives. Either I must leave the country, or go to Morazán, where the compas were gathering to form the military rearguard for the insurrection.

In the community we all gave it a lot of thought together as to what to do. Some people said to me:

'Look here, padre. You go abroad, it's too dangerous for you here. They will kill you for sure. It's up to us here to sort out our own problems.'

But others told me:

'Look, you've always spoken so well, you know how to put things just right. What you're feeling now, this fear of the repression, is what we've lived with all our lives. We've been working with you as Christians, we've been getting organised, they're giving us hell with the repression, and now all of a sudden we've got to go underground... And what are you going to do now? Are you going to leave? Of course, you're perfectly entitled to do so. You're a foreigner, and it's your right. But we have to stay here...'

What a challenge! For me, with my reputation for being so brave and demanding so much commitment from people...

I prayed a good deal before reaching a decision. The idea of my going to Morazán with the compas who were organising the war front came from the compas themselves. But it was something I wanted, too. It happened like this because in our communities there were always members of all the different popular organisations. We always supported all of them, as a matter of principle. I used to say mass as much for the FAPU people as for the Leagues or the members of the Bloque... We talked to all of them. But gradually we had been getting closer to the Popular Leagues, i.e. the ERP. Especially because of their line on unity. From the beginning their position was to fight for unity.

Some years earlier the ERP had been a very difficult lot. Because of their militarist standpoint. I had quite a few rows with them about that. They demanded that I do things I couldn't possibly do — and that I didn't want to do, for that matter. For example, they once asked me for a list of all our Christians so that they could get in touch with them and send them weapons. They kept pushing their line about a popular insurrection at any moment! I always refused to do anything like that.

'I can't possibly give you such a list. I couldn't do it without asking people first. I cannot give you a list of names!'

I refused a good many of their demands, point blank. One compa, Mateo, said in desperation:

'We'll never get anywhere with these Christians!'

'Well, if we're never going to get anywhere, we might as well stop talking now. It's been very nice knowing you, but that's an end to it, because I just can't do what you're asking.'

Bit by bit they changed their attitude. I forget now which year it was, but held an evaluation, and even admitted the mistakes they had made in the killing of Roque Dalton.* They made a severe self-criticism. Afterwards, Mateo came to see me.

'Well, Rogelio, we've had a real week of it, with all the repression... You're a Christian community, what are you going to do about it? How will you react?'

This was a completely different approach, wasn't it? I told him that we could hold a public mass to denounce what had happened, that we could stage a demonstration, and that we could occupy a church in protest...

'Carry on!'

Things had changed. Mateo would arrive and give me a political report and ask me what we could do. He didn't just roll up and demand that we do this or that. So we got on better. Later, I came across Mateo here in Morazán, and he was killed fighting in Corinto.

It was this bond between us, which gradually grew up over the years, that led them to suggest I go with them to Morazán. By the end of 1980 there was a spirit of euphoria amongst the popular organisations. They were convinced that the insurrection they were preparing would be decisive, that the war would be a short one, and that victory was within their grasp. I had considerable doubts about this. I couldn't understand how the war was going to be so short while the government had the backing of the US. I remember talking about this with Comandante Mariana, when I was discussing with her whether to go to Morazán. But the euphoria was catching, and I too shared the enthusiasm of that moment. I never imagined that the war would go on for so long.

It was a time for decisions. The compas insisted:

'You can do one of two things. But you cannot stay on here in San Salvador. Either you leave the country and join the international solidarity movement, or you come with us to the war front, to Morazán. It's up to you to decide what you want to do.'

*Roque Dalton, El Salvador's best-known writer and poet, joined the ERP in the early 1970s. Following bitter factional infighting, he was murdered in May 1975 on the orders of the ERP leadership [Ed.].

They said the same thing to all of us. We thought it over and discussed it among ourselves. There was a fraternal exchange of ideas, a collective view to enable each one to take his own decision. The others supported us, whatever decision we might reach. As a pastoral team, this was how we did it. With respect for one another, weighing up the pros and the cons...

I had one advantage over Father Pedro and Father Luis. I had been working in San Salvador for far longer, for ten years. Pedro had been deported some years previously and had been out of the country a long time. Then he had come back for a while, but... Luis had only recently arrived. They were more distressed than I was. What was more, just at the time when we were considering what to do, Pedro and Luis were going along in the car one day (at that stage we still had the car), when they noticed that they were being followed by a vehicle with smoked-glass windows of the kind the death squads use. They hurried on, with the other car on their tail. This kind of thing often happened in El Salvador. That's how they killed people, or gave them a fright. Pedro and Luis managed to escape, losing themselves in the traffic. But it was the straw that broke the camel's back. It gave them a tremendous fright.

'No, Rogelio. They are going to kill us here...'

They were afraid. I was afraid, too, but I wasn't as upset as them. Somehow I've never really believed that they were going to kill me, I don't know why. I was freer to make my decision, because I wasn't so afraid.

In the end Luis and Pedro left the country to join the international solidarity movement. We backed their decision.

All of us felt that this was a crucial moment, the moment to prove that we were close to the people. At the same time, we thought we were saying goodbye for only a few months, a short while. After that would come the victory.

I prayed a good deal during this time. There were these two possiblities, but I said to myself: 'What can I do "on the international level"? Me? What nonsense!' I felt completely useless at that sort of work, because it would involve public speaking. And what on earth would I say? 'No, I'm no good at that sort of thing. I would do better to stay here. I'll stay with my people, and go to Morazán.'

I took my decision in the chapel of the San Salvador seminary, where I was in hiding.

## Sixteen stone

The compas had proposed that I go to Morazán as a priest. They never said I had to go as a combatant, or join the guerrillas, or undertake any military mission. And to this day they have never tried to divert me to any tasks besides those of a priest.

I remember talking this over with Teodoro.

'You're going as a priest. See what you can do there as a priest. Because there are lots of Christians there in Morazán, and the combatants, too, are Christians. We know that you priests have set up study groups here in Zacamil. See if you can organise groups like that there, as well, and work out how to do it.'

I liked the idea. It seemed an important thing to do. I think the compas were very smart to recognise the importance of having a priest to accompany the people in this war, which was a people's war, a war of the poor.

If someone had asked me in 1970 or in 1972 to go to Morazán, to the war front, I would never have gone. I wouldn't have gone for fear, and because I didn't really understand the situation properly. But it's true, too, that at the time I thought my decision was just for a few months. I never imagined that the war could go on so long. No one did.

One Sunday before Christmas 1980, they took me to one of the organisation's safe houses to prepare for the journey here. Pedro and Luis had already departed. That Sunday I celebrated mass in the morning and said farewell to the people. They thought that I, too, had decided to leave.

'Of course, Father. Here they are sure to kill you. It's much better you go somewhere else.'

'That's right. But don't forget us.'

I was dying to tell them: I'm not going. I'm staying here with you. I felt rather sad. That afternoon I celebrated mass in Santiago Texacuangos. It was the same again: that I was leaving the country... and all the goodbyes. We returned to San Salvador, and I had just time to pack my suitcase for a rendezvous at 7 p.m. in the Boulevard de los Héroes. It was all very cloak and dagger. A car would draw up, they would call my name and I must get in quickly... When at last the car came, I found that they were old friends of mine, long-standing members of the Christian communities. Their duty was looking after a safe house for the organisation. There I stayed for a few days, until Christmas. On

36

Christmas Eve we had a party with the family. The next day I began my journey to the front.

We left the house by car to a rendezvous in Colonia Miramonte. There they were waiting for us, another car came, we got in and set off for San Miguel. I was travelling with Santiago, an announcer from Radio Venceremos, and Gustavo, who was also on his way to join up. In San Miguel we stayed in another house. We spent the time singing Christian songs with the owner of the house. Santiago was afraid the neighbours would notice something out of the ordinary with so much singing going on.

From there they took us to Santa Rosa de Lima. When we reached a certain footpath we had to get out. The long walk began. A guerrilla, a real youngster, offered a weapon to Santiago, and one to me. I said no, I didn't carry weapons.

From Santa Rosa we had to walk to Hecho Andrajos. For me that journey was a real calvary. I weighed nearly sixteen stone at the time, and although I thought I could walk well enough, I was sadly mistaken. After the first mile I twisted an ankle. What agony! I told the compa who was our guide, but he took no notice. My ankle was getting more and more swollen, and I couldn't bear it. By the time we reached Hecho Andrajos I was a complete wreck. My feet were bleeding, I was drenched in sweat, and in agony. I rested for a few moments and already they were telling us to get up, that we must go on to La Esperanza. Another calvary.

I was so ashamed! I had come with the idea of giving encouragement to the compas! And all the compas were looking at me pityingly. A priest so fat he can't even walk... I felt useless. Good Lord, I'm just going to be a burden. I won't be able to do anything here. In La Esperanza they asked me to celebrate mass, and that bucked me up a bit.

At that first mass I celebrated at the war front, I said something roughly like this:

'You aren't carrying rifles because you are people of violence, or because you wish to kill. In your hands, the rifle has become a sacred weapon to obtain the liberation of the people.'

They had never heard anything like that before! They were astonished that a priest should say such things. I was able to encourage them a bit.

The next morning they found a mule to take me as far as the Sapo River. They thought that the enemy had made an incursion on the other side of the river, so we went very cautiously. And I was more than a little afraid. Afterwards we found out that there was no danger. Then we had to walk again, to El Escondido. My foot was swollen, in a terrible state. From the Sapo River to Guacamaya it was a horrible journey on a really difficult path. My doubts getting stronger all the while. I was never going to be able to stand this life...

When we reached camp, the compas received me warmly, but I could see that they felt sorry for me. They even found me a rope bed of the sort the peasants use to rest on. But I slept very badly that night. I didn't sleep at all. I thought I was the biggest failure in the world. Why on earth had I come to Morazán?

## Tortillas and beans

Morazán, you see, is a hilly place. It's a region of small hills and ravines. It's a great wilderness, but there are no big mountains here, just hills and ravines. Perquín, San Fernando, Torola, Joateca, Arambala, Corinto further south, Jocoaitique... those are the big towns. 'Towns'! They're tiny places, no more than villages really, with little houses of adobe, perhaps a few of brick. A tiny school, the mayor's office, the military post, the chapel. Narrow cobbled streets in the centre. Bombing has ruined these towns. The houses have been destroyed, and there are bullet scars everywhere. Some are completely empty, where the people have fled. Others are still populated. Torola has been virtually flattened. There's just rubble and ruins there. It's tragic to see these towns, with the undergrowth gradually encroaching on them from all sides. There are the towns, and then the hamlets, smaller still, with little shacks of wood or thatch.

There's plenty of water in Morazán. That's one big advantage. When there are power cuts because the compas have sabotaged the line somewhere, it's no problem for us. We never have electric light anyway. Just candles, and occasionally an oil lamp. But we always have water. There are dozens of rivers and streams, and pools to bathe in. There are beautiful birds, birds I had never seen in San Salvador, birds of every colour, really beautiful.

There are armadillos and iguanas, too. The compas hunt them to eat. There's a type of snake, a great fat thing, which they eat too. There's fruit, as well. We find bananas, mangoes, and avocados in season.

It took me a long time to get used to the food. I've always been a bit of a glutton, I suppose. Here there's precious little to gorge yourself on. When I was in San Salvador, the one thing I never liked about Salvadorean food was the tortilla. As far as I was concerned it had no flavour at all. But, as we were in San Salvador, we could get French bread! We always had French bread with our meals. When I got to Morazán, I had to eat tortilla. There wasn't anything else. I can still remember the first meal they brought me: a handful of beans on two tortillas, to eat in your fingers. I'd never eaten with my fingers! At first it was all I could do to eat a single tortilla, with a few beans. I didn't like it. For the whole of the first month I always left the second tortilla, and ate only one. Even then I had to force it down. By the second month, I was eating two tortillas. In the end, if they gave me three, so much the better! And the tortillas we make here are good and thick!

At the front, you don't gobble your food. You learn to savour it slowly. After a whole day walking, sweating, getting covered in mud, soaked by the rain and battered by a storm, you arrive at camp and a *compañera* says:

'We've got a little coffee here.'

It's maize coffee, but it's hot. It tastes so good! Or a hot tortilla. It's the most delicious thing in the world.

...Rogelio Ponseele, a priest, who worked for ten years setting up Christian base communities in San Salvador, has now joined the Eastern Front of the Farabundo Martí National Liberation Front. In a few moments our comrade and priest Rogelio Ponseele will speak to all our brothers and sisters in El Salvador and throughout the world who are listening at this moment to Radio Venceremos, the radio station of the FMLN. *Compañero* Rogelio Ponseele.

To the people of El Salvador ... The hour of the decisive battle has arrived. Sick of so much suffering, the people have decided to rise up in arms to win their freedom. Right is on the side of the people. It is a war that has been forced on them by those who have kept them in such misery and degradation for so long... The popular army faces a difficult struggle... These honest men, the great majority of them Christians, have come forward to defend the people, whose suffering is unparalleled in history. Violence is legitimate when it is used in self-defence, and still more so when it is used to defend an entire people. Brothers and sisters, at this decisive moment... (Transcription (inaudible in places) of the words of Fr Rogelio Ponseele, speaking on Radio Venceremos, 10 January 1981, the day the general offensive was launched in El Salvador).

# 3

# *At the front*

When I first arrived my work was not very co-ordinated. And I felt a bit lonely. I realised that the compas wanted me here, to accompany them, to accompany the people, but it was up to me to work out how to do it. What's more it was at the time when they were preparing for the general offensive, in January 1981. Everything revolved around that.

With this offensive, which as it turned out was the initial rather than the final one, the war began. The war is not over yet. It drags on and on. In March came the invasion of Morazán by the army. I was trying to join in with everything. I cleaned the camp, I carried water for the compas, I took them their meals in the firing line... I was taking them their meals three times a day in the middle of a mortar attack. It was a very heavy bombardment at La Guacamaya. The compas appreciated what I was doing but after a few days they told me that this was not my job, and I was expressly and emphatically forbidden to do it!

At that time my idea was to join in any work going. I dug air raid shelters, shifted earth, did whatever there was to do. After the invasion we moved to a zone called El Centro. Holy Week was coming and the compas took Villa El Rosario on Good Friday. There we celebrated the mass of the resurrection.

The enemy wanted to recover the ground they had lost. This was the first bombing of civilians I experienced. It was very cruel. When they shell the camp, it's not so bad, because things are always spread out a bit and one mortar-bomb falls here, another there and it's not so frightening. But when you see a mortar attack on such a tiny village... And they were people who had never experienced anything like this, they were terrified.

41

'Father, what's going to happen to us?'

'How long are these mortars going to keep coming?'

'Will they leave us alone after this?'

Days of non-stop mortar attacks. We gathered everyone together in one place, in one big house, and all slept on the floor. The children cried and cried, but not because they were afraid of the bombs. It was because of the parasites which gave them stomach-ache. I couldn't sleep that night. I sat up and watched them. My God, what poverty! And the bombs whistling overhead. Whee! Boooomb! And all the time hoping that the bomb would not fall on the house and kill us all.

It was a mistake of mine to gather everyone in one place. Afterwards I learned that it is better to disperse them. I had no experience either. I spent the night watching them. Those poor women weighed down with young children, desperate with anxiety, the children so emaciated, hungry, crying... I'll never forget that scene of anguish. I'll always remember that night. I just watched and watched them. When I think of that night, it always reminds me of the question I get asked so often:

'Father, what's God up to? Don't you say that God acts? And how does God act, Father?'

During an air raid you think about death, you feel it close, it comes through the air. Bombing makes you nervous. In Morazán there is the permanent threat of death by bombing, military invasion, an enemy landing in the area, a mortar attack, a stray bullet... I'm someone who feels fear. One day I thought I couldn't go on living with the anguish of thinking that I was going to die. In San Salvador I'd already had some pretty bad moments, I suppose. And I'd made a little progress towards accepting death. But it's here in Morazán that I've really had to face up to it. So many people die and I may die too. I am neither more nor less than anyone else. I'm not worth more, and I'm not worth less...

You have to avoid death if you can, but you must learn to live with the consciousness that it might come tomorrow, and not be paralysed by that. It's difficult. When you lose the fear of death you begin to feel a tremendous calm. Then when the bombing starts you can keep cool, you can make decisions and you keep your nerve. You reaffirm your commitment: to be ready to give your life. And so you survive these moments. Your nerves can kill you even before a bomb does, you know.

I think it's important to learn to make death an integral part of our vision of life. All of us want to do something great, but not to die, please! That's why I've never liked one of the slogans the compas use: 'Victory or death!' Salvadoreans, the compas, our Christians, are not like that. Death is part of their vision of life. The Salvadoreans have taught me that I too must make it part of mine. I, who talk so much about Jesus' death, his sacrifice on the cross, was trying to avoid death at all costs. I hadn't understood a thing. But here I have learned from the Salvadoreans to make death a part of life.

## Our mass is a party
After the taking of the Villa El Rosario, we went back to the camp where Radio Venceremos was working. Now I began to work in a more formal way. Every Sunday I said mass in the chapel at El Zapotal. The locals came and the compas. That's how I began my pastoral work, gathering the people to celebrate the eucharist.

### Mass under a rain of shells and bullets
On 24 March, after two weeks of fighting, when the enemy fire was at its worst, the Frente Command decided to celebrate the first anniversary of the murder of Archbishop Romero. To celebrate a mass and a political and cultural event with local people from the area, right in the middle of the offensive! And we did it. The civilian population were gathered in the hamlet of El Mozote and the meeting took place literally under a rain of mortar shells and machine-gun fire from helicopters. The people and their revolutionary army paid homage to Archbishop Romero in the midst of an offensive.

Radio Venceremos was there and it really was one of the most beautiful programmes we have ever produced. It was an opportunity to show plainly our own military strength and the impotence of the enemy army. We had announced several days previously that we were going to hold the mass and where, and even named the time. In the event, the enemy army tried to prevent us, and to take advantage of the concentration of people and guerrilla forces at a known spot to strike a heavy blow against us, but they failed completely.

In fact, while we were at mass, which we were transmitting live, they concentrated their artillery fire on us, their helicopters machine-gunned us, and their infantry made a supreme effort to break through our defences and attack the place where the event was taking place. But more than our fire-power, more than the number of our forces, it was the determination and sacrifice of our troops who kept the enemy at bay during the entire celebration, and for the whole duration of the offensive.

They could not frighten off the civilian population, who were paying homage to their murdered pastor. They could not silence the priest Fr Rogelio Ponseele (sic), who denounced the assassins of Archbishop Romero, the same ones who are murdering the people. They could not silence Radio Venceremos, which transmitted to our people and the world this moving homage of a people in struggle to one of their most beloved martyrs. (Testimony of 'a member of Collective III' of Radio Venceremos, Published in *Señal de Libertad*, 1983, 24.

I've always been able to celebrate mass here at the front. I've never had to suspend the celebration because of bombing. Sometimes I've not been able to go to a particular community because the situation is difficult in this or that area. If the mass is in a community in Morazán, which is territory controlled by the FMLN, there's no problem, although there's always a lookout, and people on guard. If the mass is in a village, in Corinto for instance, which the enemy can get to more quickly, then the compas send a column on ahead. One patrol here, another there, to protect the service, so we are not taken by surprise. They always say to me:

'No Rogelio, you are not going alone, we'll send a few *compañeros* with you.'

And they get annoyed if I go and do something in some community without telling them beforehand. They're defending religious freedom, you see. Of course it wouldn't help them if anything were to happen to me. But it's not just for that. They have a deep respect for the people's faith. And they're really glad that religious services are being held.

Mass is a time for celebration, a festival for everyone. We celebrate whenever we can, whether it's Sunday or not. People arrive from their villages and hamlets, wearing their best clothes. And however poor the community is, there's always a festive spirit and things to sell. They sell bread, or bananas, or a watermelon, that sort of thing. Or they make cold drinks.

When I have an alb, I wear it. Sometimes I don't have one because I've lost it. I always wear the stole, which gives the mass a more festive character. We can turn any place into a church. A tree, a little table, table-cloths, flowers... I'm always moved by the way people come before the service to tell me the names of their dead, so that I can offer the mass for them. I always take a notebook.

'Write down the name of my father, my mother, my three little brothers, my granny, my uncle...'

They're all like this.. And these names are never of people who died of illness. They've been killed, they died in a massacre or an air raid. Sometimes out of a whole page in my notebook there are only one or two names of people whose death was 'an act of God'. That's what they say of someone who has died of an illness: it was 'an act of God'. But so many have been murdered, so many...

The mass is simple. Bible readings and then discussion together. A bible text and three simple questions to help them draw out the relationship between the bible and their own lives. They say:

'That's just what's happening today. It's the same!'

They're absolutely delighted when they discover that what's written in the bible is just what they are experiencing, what they are doing. It gives them strength. The bible is the most beautiful book there is, because you can open it at any page and they'll' say, 'Why, it's just like us!' For learning to understand their own history, the people couldn't hope for a better book than the bible, don't you think?

Sometimes at mass we have Los Torogoces. They are a musical group. They live in camp but if they can get to the community where we are celebrating mass they come to sing. It's a bonus if they come, and makes the mass jollier. We often sing the Nicaraguan *Misa Campesina* and we add some songs from the *Misa Salvadoreña*. We like 'You are the God of the Poor' a lot. Sometimes when I'm walking up hill and down dale, it's three or four hours before I come to a community along the way. In the few houses still standing I hear children and grown-ups singing: 'You are the God of the poor, the down-to-earth human God, God who sweats in the street...' We've been singing this song ever since I got to Morazán. People really like it.

Los Torogoces have the job of livening up the mass. There are six of them. They have a drum, guitars, a violin, a double bass, and an accordion. Originally none of them could play the accordion but they 'rescued' one from a house and now they play it. None of them can read music but they can play anything. They play the violin like great musicians. All by ear. I can read music and I can't play a thing. They can't read but they can play anything.

When I first arrived, the Torogoces weren't around. I was looking for someone to play during mass. I met Felipe, who played the violin. When people talk about hatred I always think of Felipe. The army killed his wife, his mother-in-law and five children. All together, in a single massacre. He has two other children who are with him at the front, fighting. But there is no hatred in Felipe. There is determination to fight, but no hatred.

I've met so many people who have managed to turn such terrible moral anguish into a fighting spirit rather than into hatred. That is why it makes me laugh when bishops speak of forgiveness in their pastoral letters. Do they know what they are talking about?

I think, for instance, of Octavio Ortiz's father. They killed his priest son, and they killed his other son, who was finishing his bachelor's degree. And his brother. They burnt the body and their mother had to gather up the pieces to bury it. Now he has had news that two of his children have fallen in combat here at the front. His wife is in a refuge in San Salvador, his mother in a refuge in Nicaragua, some of his daughters are trying to find work in San Salvador, others in the USA. The whole family has been torn apart. And with all that death and sorrow he says to me that we must not hate, that we must forgive and God will give us strength to do it. But he doesn't just repeat that automatically, it really comes from his heart. He doesn't hate. That is why I think, what are some bishops and priests talking about when they speak of forgiveness? What do they know about it?

Many compas who come to mass have scruples about going to communion because they have been in a battle, have fired their weapons and killed people. They feel bad about it. Although they don't all admit it, they feel it. They come to mass, they take part, but they don't come up to communion. I always insist that they shouldn't worry. The fact that they are fighting and are prepared to lay down their lives isn't just words, it's reality. It's the greatest commitment anyone can have, the most Christian commitment. Because they are prepared to give their lives for others they have every right to come to communion. I tell them this and I am convinced that it is right.

So our mass is a party. A community festival. When I've been to Europe, oh, those masses in Europe make you want to cry! In Zacamil, too, mass was festive, joyous, everyone took part. Once when I went back to Belgium they asked me to celebrate mass in Louvain, in a very ancient and important church. They put me behind a great altar and I had to wear all the gear, the chasuble, the lot! And I was about fifty yards away from the people! I couldn't preach, I couldn't find words. I had prepared well and yet I didn't know what to say. I was thinking, what am I doing here? What on earth is the meaning of this? I've never needed to ask that question when I celebrate mass here under a tree with the people.


## The real priest

I never go to the front line. They don't let me. And I don't carry a weapon. I never have. I believe it's better that way. Sometimes the compas tease me and say:

'Come on, Rogelio, grab a rifle!'

But not when they're being serious. They're quite clear about it. They know that different people have different jobs.

'So what's my job, then?'

'Rogelio, your job is to go round the communities and do pastoral work. You just being here with us, celebrating mass, forming bible study groups, is enough. That's what we want you to do. That's your job.'

When I arrived in Morazán most people hadn't seen a priest for ages. I didn't even know where to begin. There were the guerrilla camps, and the civilian population. I didn't know a single catechist. I had come to... to do what, I wondered! That is what it was like at the beginning. But I was in demand everywhere. The people found out that a priest had arrived and they wanted to see him. I began to travel on foot to one place after another and people took me to their villages to celebrate mass and above all to baptise. As there had been no priest in the area for a long time and the birth-rate is very high, there were a lot of children, older ones as well as babies, who had not been baptised.

People came to fetch me on horseback, out of respect. In many places it is the custom to fetch the priest on horseback. A peasant leads the horse with a halter and two others walk, one on either side, as an escort. They couldn't imagine a priest arriving on foot with a backpack.

One day the parish priest from Anamorós was expected in a community near Corinto. I was there in that community, the village having been taken by the compas. Most of the people in this community are with us, but there is a group of traditionalists who try to keep out of the war. I knew this priest was arriving, so I went to see him. I wanted to see a brother priest, I really wanted to talk to him. I walked for at least four hours with my backpack to get there. I arrived at eight o'clock. The other priest arrived at ten. I was chatting with people when I heard someone shout:

'The priest is coming!'

I was surprised and said to them:

'The priest's here.'

'No, no, the priest!'

Meaning the 'real' priest. He arrived on horseback with an escort of two and the one who was leading the horse. He arrived wearing a white cassock. The little group of pious villagers flocked round him, pleased as could be to see him like that. I went up to him.

'Father, I'd like to concelebrate with you. You preach and if you like I can say a few words...'

'No, no, some other time you can say what you like. But today I am going to say the mass.'

'I only want to say a few words, to greet these people. I know them.'

I was trying to find some common ground with him, some unity. In the end he accepted. But he didn't preach at all, he just let me speak. He didn't want to say a single word in my presence. That's prejudice. Some people think I'm a priest who has gone off the rails.

He heard confessions before the mass. And at communion he gave hosts only to people who had confessed to him. He had been counting them, with a rosary! Anyone he had not counted, who had not been to confession to him, he would not give them communion: 'I know exactly how many of you can receive communion!'

The people stared at each other. Nor would he give communion to the guerrillas from the community, who had come to mass with their guns as they always do. The *compañeros* were highly scandalised.

I have to say that relations with some priests are very difficult. There are huge differences between us.

When I was in San Salvador I had to fight quite often in clergy meetings. I've always been a bit argumentative. In a letter I once wrote from here to a fellow priest I told him I needed quarrels like that, that I missed the clergy meetings, and all that.

Does Archbishop Rivera support me? I would say yes, but in his own way... We have an advantage: what we are doing, accompanying the poor, sharing their lives and troubles, doing this pastoral work of accompanying, trying to give hope, all this kind of thing... well it's going to be difficult for a bishop to disapprove of that, isn't it? At least, if he's going to be honest

48

about it. And I do think Archbishop Rivera is honest. When I say he supports me in his own way, it's because sometimes we feel he's close to us and sometimes rather distant. We were very happy when he said that God's word must be announced to everyone, everywhere. That means at the war fronts too, doesn't it? He didn't use those exact words, but in one of his sermons he said something like that and that's what we took him to mean.

I personally felt very pleased when he shared with me in a celebration of the word on Guazapa Mountain. On that occasion he was subtly giving me to understand that he agreed with what I was doing. One becomes sensitive to these things. They cheer us up after five years of feeling so isolated from communion in the church we used to be so involved in.

In Morazán I am in the diocese of San Miguel. The bishop here is Alvarez. But I have nothing to do with him. Nothing. He is a colonel in the army; he holds the rank.

At the beginning I was 'the little father'. At the beginning. Now the compas address me familiarly as 'vos' and even feel free to swear at me sometimes! I have a very warm relationship with the compas. At the beginning if there was a better bed, it was for the 'little father'. If there was a tortilla, it was for the 'little father'. Gradually this stopped. They felt more at home with me and I was no longer the 'little father'. We were sleeping in the same place, eating together what little there was to eat. I think this is a very deep experience, because however simply we appear to live, we priests always have a certain degree of power. We have a house, money, a car... We have power, which is why the people come to us. Can you help me, father? Can you give this sick person a lift in your car? And the priest lends the car or drives to the hospital himself. We have power, we have advantages, we have privileges.

In San Salvador I went to La Fosa shanty town and ate the 'little tortillas' with the people. In the slums tortilla was all there was, and small ones at that. But when I got home we opened the refrigerator, took out a chicken and a large cold drink! Here I queue up with the compas for a few sips of cold juice, just a little because there is no sugar, sometimes only just enough to wet your lips. And you know that has to last you the whole day... It's so easy to share people's lives for one or two hours. Here it is permanent.

At the front I have nothing. Nothing for myself and nothing to give to anyone else. You are on the same level as the compa who has nothing — neither do you. Here I sometimes feel I am nobody.

I go about with my backpack like everyone else, with nothing. What can this priest offer them? I have nothing. All I can do is accompany them, and share with them this little faith of mine. There's no power here. My church is a tree, a bit of shade, a table-cloth. So the priest is nobody because he has nothing. I don't even have the power to help them!

## Base communities

It was time to start work in the communities. So I started to run courses over several days like those we had set up in San Salvador. I would meet with the people who were going to promote the communities, the catechists and delegates of the word. In Morazán I came across quite a few men who had been catechists years before. We made a plan of work with them, and looked at some of the details involved in getting started. Now in the whole area of Morazán we have 50 catechists, but only a few of these have had a proper training. The catechists visit the communities when we have to be away for a while, going from place to place because of the war. It's the catechists who get the community to come to discussion group meetings, or to a celebration of the word or to mass, when I can get there to celebrate it.

The community meets with the delegate of the word. These are peasants who can barely read. They take ages to read out a passage from the bible and I, who am so impatient, sometimes get restless. I start worrying whether the people are understanding it, if they take so long over it, and whether they're getting bored. The delegates not only take ages over the reading, they also preach at great length. The truth is that this is only my worry. The people understand and they like it. In simple words, with little examples, the delegates explain everything. It's me they sometimes don't understand, because there are always differences of language and there is such a wide cultural gap...

One day I was visiting a community with a delegate of the word. As we were coming home he asked me:

'Father, why do you say that we mustn't be pessimistic?'

'Because we must be optimists.'

'But Father, why do you say "pessimistic"? What do you mean?.
I know a *pecenista* is a member of that party... But I don't understand why you keep telling us not to join that party, because here no one belongs to it...' For heaven's sake! For him *pesimista* meant *pecenista*, a member of the PCN, the party of the military!

50

If he didn't understand me, even though he was going about with me all the time, what about the rest? Sometimes I'm left wondering whether anybody understands a word I say.

When I had been at the front for just over a year another priest came to work here in Morazán, Father Miguel Ventura, a Salvadorean. In the early seventies he had done a lot of work in this region, doing consciousness raising and setting up base communities. A few years ago he was captured and tortured. He felt he had no support from his bishop or from the other priests in the region at the time. He left the country and went to the US. The danger there of course is that you gradually start to settle down. He worked in the solidarity movement, and with refugees, learned English, but he was beginning to settle down.

In 1981 he found out that I was here in Morazán and began to ask himself questions. He started to feel uncomfortable. Then he went to Nicaragua and the *compañeros* showed him some films they had of the front here. When he saw practically all his people, whom he had trained, who were now comandantes in the FMLN, working here, he apparently said:

'Right, no more films!'

And off he went to think things over. He began to think about coming back. In 1982 he arrived here. He knew Morazán better than me. He knew every path in the region. When we went to the villages together, *compañeros* would appear on every corner to greet him:

'Miguel, you've come back!'

And they hugged him. Meeting his people again was really moving. And he decided to stay. We are friends, *compañeros*.

Miguel has taught me patience. I'm a very impatient person, I always have been. He's helped me to treat people more calmly. He comes from peasant stock, a very deep man, a real priest.

'No, Rogelio, it's better for the delegate of the word to read the lesson, the people will understand him. It's more important he does it than someone who knows it all.'

I still have a lot to learn from the Salvadoreans. With Miguel I can also talk over a lot of things to do with the faith. At the beginning, I felt lonely. Not alone, because I was surrounded by lots of very warm and affectionate people, but who could I talk to about my faith, and my doubts about it? You see, my faith is not like that of the peasants. I can talk to Miguel, he understands me very well and he likes talking to me. I pray with him and we meditate together. He is a great support. We support one another, you see. As well as us two priests, there are the catechists, and two other workers, Paty and Foncho. Not many. Too few, with all that needs to be done.

Our pastoral work with the local people in the communities has now been divided up into five areas of work: the celebration of the word and the celebration of the eucharist, discussion groups, human rights, children's catechism classes, and support for community projects.

The big one is the eucharist. The discussion groups are important as well. I think perhaps this is the most important work we are doing, because it's fundamental to ensure that there isn't a great gap between strong political commitment and Christian vision. Over the whole zone we now have come 50 discussion groups, with quite a number of people in each of them.

People meet to read the bible, to discuss, sing and pray. In some places we are more successful than in others. Sometimes the peasants are afraid of joining a group like this because when the army comes they are accused of being guerrillas.

We look for texts that arouse hope, help them understand their history, their sufferings, and texts which encourage them to participate in everything to do with the community.

I have no scruples about encouraging the people to participate in the revolutionary process, the armed struggle. To me it seems so obvious. And to them too. Their war is such a just and legitimate one. That is why they find it so hard to understand how a bishop or a priest can be against this war. They don't understand it, because for them a bishop or a priest is the most important person in the world.

Once I tried to stir things up in the discussion:

'Listen, Radio Venceremos criticised Bishop Gregorio Rosa Chávez. I don't think they should be doing this, because our pastors are our pastors and we have to respect them.'

I wanted to see what they would say. Because for them Radio Venceremos is something sacred and the radio should not be criticised. But a bishop is also something sacred. A dilemma, wasn't it? But do you know, they resolved the issue in favour of the bishop! These were well-trained people, catechists. They even tried to write to Radio Venceremos to ask it please not to speak badly of the bishop.

'If the bishop speaks against us, it is not because that's what he really thinks. He's doing it for his own safety. If he criticises us, it's for safety's sake, because they could kill him. But the truth is he is with us.'

That's what they think. They never understand that a priest or a bishop could be against their struggle, against their war. They have always lived in poverty and the army comes to kill them. What should they do? Take up arms and defend themselves, fight! That's obvious. Things like this are always coming up in our discussion groups.

We're also doing some work on human rights. We have to be close to the people suffering most, those who are victims of bombing and military raids. We visit these people, we talk to them, we see that they've at least got a bit of maize. If the husband has been captured and his wife is left alone with the children and there's no maize, then they can't make tortillas, so what are they going to eat? We also collect information about captures and murders, in order to denounce them within El Salvador and also internationally.

Then there's the catechism for the children. They learn with the bible: Abraham, Moses, the wilderness, Jesus... They have their little discussions and games and songs. Finally, we try to collaborate in all the projects the communities are working on. We are at war and they are all survival projects. There are production co-operatives for beans, maize, rice; vegetable plots; health with preventive and curative medicine, little shops, consumer co-operatives, schools for the children.

Around these projects the community is organised and the neighbourhood council is formed. The FMLN appoints the political leader. He is a peasant representative of the community, respected by the people. He is the one to make decisions in case of danger, the communication link from above to below. He conveys the concerns of those below to those above. There are meetings, the people discuss and make plans. The political leader is trusted a great deal. He is a father to the community. They accept him. It's his job to win more and more confidence from people and if he fails the FMLN change him. This is not a perfect democracy but it is the beginnings of democracy.

The Christian communities are represented in the neighbourhood council. We support all these projects. We do what we can. The little schools are half-wrecked houses, with a few stones for the children to sit on and a plank to put their exercise books on. We teach the children to read. And a little of the geography of Morazán, their own environment. We also teach them about the FMLN, its organisation and where the war fronts are, the geography of El Salvador, a little history, the events of 1932, their own history...

The adults also have classes. I've taken part in various literacy campaigns. We have guerrilla *compañeros* who have to carry out important missions and yet who can neither read nor write. There are comandantes who are great military strategists, but who can hardly string a couple of letters together. It's a serious drawback because they have to receive messages, look after communications, duties, etc.

They have plenty of motivation to learn. At one time the *compañeros* stubbornly insisted that we had to teach literacy by the consciousness-raising method of Freire. But I insisted that we needed something lighter: pa-pe-pi-po-pu and la-le-li-lo-lu and word-formation and so on. The traditional method, because it was urgent for them to learn and the compas had enough political education anyway. And they learn very fast because they want to learn.

I have taught a number of guerrillas to read. Sometimes I got discouraged because they didn't learn as quickly as I expected. But a year later I would meet up with them:

'Father, do you remember teaching me to form my first few letters? Well now I can write.'

With great effort and starting from the basis we gave them, they had made astonishing progress. Now they can understand a written message or write one themselves. Actually I cannot understand what they write, the way they form their letters with hooks. But they understand each other. It's the other way round when a letter comes from the doctor, I'm the only one who can understand it. They can't read the doctor's writing.

# 4

# *On the run*

In December 1981 we had go on the run for a few weeks — leave the camp to avoid the enemy. The term 'liberated zone' is a very relative one. Morazán is now a liberated zone, a zone under total control, but even here we have to move about to keep out of the enemy's way.

Under control means that neither the armed forces nor the government has any structure of power here. There is no town hall, no barracks. But there are troop drops, military invasions, air raids. A drop means that first there's a bombing raid to clear the ground and then 15 or 20 helicopters come and drop troops and you find yourself face to face with the enemy in no time.

Apart from that, there's a permanent war going on. There has been since 1981. So people have to move about. For years we've been moving about. Now because of their new political tactics the army doesn't come quite so often to carry out direct massacres. They're trying to win over the population to get them away from us. They either bring them food or withhold it, as the case may be, as a form of blackmail. The people are smart, and tell the soldiers that yes, of course, they need food, and please could they bring more, because otherwise what will they do...? The people know the armed forces all too well. The people are smart: for them it's a tactic they use to gain legal status to some extent.

We go on the run. The word we use is *guindear*, which means 'to flee'. When someone is running people say 'he's on *guinda*', on the run. It has a negative tone. That is why the comandantes have said that we can't use the word any more, we have to talk about 'manoeuvres'. After all, going on the run is running away, but manoeuvring is playing with the enemy on the ground. We play with them, like children playing hide and seek.

Once I was talking with a *compañero* and I kept talking about going on the run. Behind me stood Jonas, one of the senior comandantes. He is a very fierce character. And I kept talking about going on the run.

'That's enough, Rogelio! We've already said that this word is not to be used any more. Here we talk about manoeuvring, not running.'

It comes to the same thing in the end, I thought to myself. It is the same. It means walking for whole days and nights along those paths. It means going hungry. And worst of all is when we don't find any water. Sometimes we're on the run, — sorry, 'manoeuvres'! — for two weeks solid. Sometimes longer. Always walking. An invasion comes and then those involved in the military structure meet and fight. But the population, the wounded, the priests, the supply workers, the press and publicity workers, the prisoners if there are any — anyway, a vast number of people — have to go on the run. Walking night and day, 'manoeuvring'. At first we moved in large groups but now we go in smaller groups and not just in one group, but some one way and some another. Groups of around a hundred people. Recently, people have been making more and more effort to stay put without manoeuvring. Going on the run isn't easy. Part of the population stays put. Others go on the run with their political leaders. Others, who are already experienced, go by themselves. Nowadays there's more control over what to do in each case.

In the early days we had an invasion in the south which lasted a month and a half. We had to go on the run northwards for a month and a half. A month and a half walking all day, every day. Sometimes it was more intensive than others. But it was hard. I remember when we got back to the camp I threw myself on the floor and said:

'Now don't let anyone disturb me. I am going to sleep!'

And I took my plastic ground-sheet out of my backpack, and...

'No, Rogelio, grab your pack, the enemy is coming.' There was another invasion in the north. We walked all night to the Cacahuatique hill. We stayed there in hiding for a week.

Where we walk depends on the enemy's position. We take guides who know the land with their eyes shut, every little track. We take armed *compañeros* in case defence is necessary. At first when everyone was on the run together, it was difficult. Hundreds of people, children, women, old people carrying their bits and pieces. The pots to make coffee, the tortilla pan, the mules carrying sacks of maize. The dogs went too. Everything had to be done in complete silence. Morazán dogs somehow seemed to know this and didn't bark. They are dogs that keep you company. They see a 'manoeuvre' go by and they come along too, quiet as mice.

Sometimes we can rest at night. When we are sure where the enemy are and they are giving no signs of advancing, then we sleep normally. Normally means in the open, with our precious sheets of plastic. At the front, everyone has their own 'plastic'. It's the most sacred thing we have here. The 'plastic' is your bed. You put your pack under your head for a pillow and you're okay.

On the journey the women stop to make tortillas because we take everything with us to make them. Sometimes it's hilarious. A message is passed from person to person.

'The enemy is 200 yards away.'

In a whisper. The enemy may in fact be further away but this is done to make an impression. Especially on the civilians who are not so disciplined. And the message is passed on:

'The enemy is 200 yards away.'

Not a sound, not even a footstep... And at that moment someone drops a pan and it goes crashing down. Clang! Clang! Clang! What a racket! But even so nothing has ever happened on any manoeuvre. We play games with the army and run circles round them.

When you are on the run and are discovered you have to find a safe place. Bombs are never the most dangerous thing, so long as they don't fall on top of you, of course. The most dangerous thing is the flying shrapnel. But if you are lying flat on the ground in a hole with a wall, a stone, something to act as a parapet, then you're safe from shrapnel. In the mountains everyone knows what to do. They've had years of experience.

The purpose of going on the run is to save lives when there is an air raid, an invasion or an brush with the army. We manoeuvre to save lives more than for the sake of playing games with the army. But we don't waste time even on the run. We manoeuvre southwards, so we have a meeting with the catechists in the south. Then, when we come back to the camp, it hasn't been time wasted. You always have to be ready, with your pack to hand.

What do I carry in my backpack? A piece of plastic sheeting to sleep under, a few clothes, the bible, some hosts and wine to celebrate mass.

Sometimes I don't take hosts. Then I tell the peasants:

'Jesus used bread and wine, the everyday food in his time. Our everyday food is tortilla, so that's what we'll use to celebrate.'

It's no problem for our people. They take communion with just as much devotion. It's perfectly natural and it's essential, anyway, if the people want mass and I haven't got any hosts... I know there are people who complain about 'those priests who celebrate with tortillas'. But for the people it's no problem.

Priests from nearby regions sometimes send me things: a book of liturgy or about pastoral work or a pamphlet that could be useful. And hosts and wine to celebrate mass with. Apparently in a meeting of clergy and nuns Bishop Alvarez complained that he knew very well there were priests who dared pass hosts and wine on to the war zone. He called it a crime! What rubbish! How can he fail to appreciate that in these zones too, in the midst of war, mass is celebrated with hosts and wine? He made it sound as though we were bringing in artillery! Well, as somebody once said, the people here are so religious these hosts and wine are worth more than a gun.

What's the matter with the church? I get really upset when I think about it. How is it possible that bishops and priests can be so negative towards people who are so humble, so poor, who have suffered so much and have every right to fight for a different society?

**Exodus**

On these journeys the peasants have great advantages over townspeople. Hilario, for example. I like travelling with him. At night he walks along as bold as brass, with amazing sureness of foot. During the day he sometimes falls over, but never at night. How does he do it? Some wear boots and walk the better for it. But all most of the compas have is simple rubber-soled shoes. In all the water and mud they hardly last a month. The local people have even worse shoes. It's a great problem here how to get hold of shoes when we have to walk so much...

When winter comes and the rains, the going on the run is better in one way and worse in another. Better because the enemy has difficulties. Worse because we spend night after night with rain pouring down on us, sleeping with our plastic sheet but getting soaked. If you had two plastic sheets you could put one underneath and one on top, but no one has two. That would be a great luxury here! You feel so tired you sleep anyway, even though you're wet through. It's wonderful to wake up in the morning and see sunshine. Your clothes dry out and you forget your troubles. If the sun didn't come out quickly, we'd all get ill with arthritis. But no one suffers from that here.

In winter the paths are worse to walk along. Muddy, and, when a whole column has gone on ahead, nothing but mud! I slip and fall over all the time. The *compañeros* know how to stay upright a bit better but as for me... Well, I've improved to some extent. In the beginning I fell right over: splat! I ached all over. Now I know how to fall more gracefully and it's not so bad, but I still fall over. Afterwards you have to walk along all filthy. Being so dirty has its advantages, though, because then you don't have to bother where you sit down or where you make your bed. And that's a blessing.

I don't know how many times I've been on the run. I lost count long ago. Twenty? Thirty? Sometimes it lasted for weeks on end. This has been going on since 1981. We had to go on the run right from the beginning. The only difference is that at the beginning there were civilians living there and we didn't have to go on the run so often, because the army was slower to act. Now the army keeps on coming in and we have to move about more and more. But each time we do it with fewer people, and each time we become more mobile, we get better at it. It's become a habit now.

These manoeuvres are an opportunity to hold meetings whenever we stop. We are thrown together and so we get to talk. We use the opportunity to have long talks. And talking is very important in the middle of a war. Talking helps us. Going on the run is also an opportunity to have a study session with the *compañeros*, sometimes based on a bible reading. There's always an opportunity to get work done. We're never paralysed even when we're on the road.

When we go on maonoeuvres and there's nothing to eat or nothing to drink, we think of what it says in the bible. The exodus, the wilderness, the journey of the people of God, taking the promised land... Like that people, whose journey lasted forty years. We've only been at war five years, and even so we are beginning to feel a bit tired... it's natural. People want peace. But they want a kind of peace which means a real change, not peace at any price.

We also meditate on what St Paul says, that a Christian has no permanent home here on earth. We do have. The villagers have too, though they often have to leave them. We're always on the move.

There's no fixed home here. It's hard because we priests are accustomed to having a house, a table, our books, a typewriter, tape recorder... classical music! I love classical music, Mozart, Beethoven, Rachmaninov... I've loved their music ever since I was quite small, and I've always enjoyed it. In San Salvador, in Zacamil I had my own tape recorder, quite a good one, which I seldom loaned out, so that I could listen to a bit of music from time to time. But at the front, we have no house, no table, no music, no books, no tape recorder. Nothing!

Sometimes I take a book with me in my pack: Jon Sobrino's Christology. Rather a heavy read, wouldn't you say? But I like it. I read a page under a tree. I like it. One day I came across a really important idea. The book says that only those who keep walking can have the hope of arriving one day. Only those who take part. That's what's happening today in El Salvador, as the war drags on. The war doesn't end. The·ones who feel most weary, though, are those who've remained on the sidelines, spectators to the events. They are the ones who get most weary, the ones who lose heart. But those who are on the march don't, they feel they are getting closer. In the thick of it we don't feel the tiredness so much. There's more pessimism and defeatism about the war abroad than there is here in El Salvador. And we are the ones who are at war, in the thick of it! The further away you are, the less you take part, the more you get tired. It's strange, isn't it?

When I'm on the march, I often feel in the presence of God. Especially if we have to go in silence. When we walk in single file, one behind the other, you are with others, but you are practically alone and have a chance to meditate while you walk.

I always give thanks to God. I feel privileged and I am grateful to God for giving me the opportunity to live here at this time, to be able to take part in these events, which are of such crucial importance for this people. I'm grateful to God that I can live here, with all these risks, with the compas. Sometimes people feel pity for me. Look at the guerrillas, they say, poor things, and that poor priest with them, look at the state of him! Why? Being part of this project and sharing this experience with the compas is a happiness I cannot put into words. I just give thanks to God.

## The wounded

If the manoeuvre is at night I can't see a thing. There are holes, stones. I try to keep hold of the person in front of me, so that I don't miss the path, because if you get off the path and lose the column, you are lost. At night and in silence. That's how they travel with the wounded, as well, carrying them. Imagine the pain and discomfort for the wounded person. It's tough.

Our hospitals are always provisional. They're mobile and travel from place to place, following the manoeuvre. There are a few safe ones for those wounded who can't be moved.

We take most of the wounded with us on a manoeuvre. If I had to carry one of the wounded, I couldn't stand it. It's so difficult, especially at night when you can't see where you're putting your foot and the whole time you're desperately trying not to drop the wounded person. Once I offered to carry someone and was accepted. And how long did I last? An hour. I remember one compa, a peasant, a tiny man with the body of a undernourished child. He was a catechist. On one march, he offered to carry the wounded. It was for thirty hours non-stop. Thirty hours! Up hill and down dale, across ravines and rivers... I would have died.

He told me afterwards that he had found it so hard that during the brief halts on the journey he had moved away from the others to have a good cry, his body ached so much. He had felt like running away but he had come back to take up the burden again, because you can't leave the wounded behind. The wounded are one of the *compañeros*' greatest worries. That is why we were so pleased that after Duarte's daughter was kidnapped they got so many injured people out of the country to be cared for abroad.

Eduardo is a good doctor. He's a surgeon, very competent. But he lacks proper medical equipment, there's a shortage of medicines. And not all the doctors here are as competent as he is.

'We could have saved this compa... I just didn't have such and such... Perhaps it was my fault, I didn't know how to...'

They suffer for these failures. Wounded people whose lives they couldn't save. And we lose compas who are like gold to us, who die because of all these difficulties.

At the front there are various hospitals and various clinics. If a *compañero* is very seriously injured, they try to get him out of the country to save him. Others have to recover in our hospitals. Afterwards, they rejoin the struggle. I am always amazed how after such dreadful experiences, being wounded — and wounded

61

here with all the hardships that involves — they rejoin the struggle. That's bravery for you.

Every day a *compañero* is wounded, a *compañero* falls in battle, one who arrives at the hospital half dead, one who has lost his legs, a *compañero* who goes mad. It's a tough environment. The work I find most difficult is visiting patients in the hospitals and clinics. This is a confession, by the way. I recognise that I haven't done enough of this, because these wounded *compañeros* deserve to have company, but it grieves me so much to go and see them that I nearly always try to find some other job to do.

I remember Tavo, a *compañero* hit by a mine. Eduardo was trying to save him, he had already operated seven times. I happened to pass by:

'Come in, Rogelio. It's Tavo.'

At that moment I lacked the courage to go in. I felt incapable of consoling him. What could I say?

Tavo died that night and I never saw him again. I was angry with myself and I still have this weight on my conscience. I feel such pain when I go to see the wounded. Perhaps someone who has lost both legs... I am with him and say a few words and when I come out I realise it was he who cheered me up, not vice versa.

'Let's keep going, Father. If I get out of here, they will always find something for me to do.'

What courage! And me with scarcely enough courage to go and see him... I know this is my weak point. It's not that I'm a wimp, but such great pain leaves me paralysed. And war is cruel.

### Life and death

When I'm with a compa who's going to die, I hardly ever speak to him about God. It's an unconscious omission. It's not that I tell myself, 'I'm not going to talk about God'. But I just can't bring myself to. I just try to be near the dying person, to hold his hand and be with him. This is the only thing I can do. Miguel is much better at this than me. He knows how to talk about God at such times. And that helps the compa. But I can't, I don't know how to. And I try to run away, escape. There is a very fine doctor who does not share our Christian faith but whenever a compa is dying he invites us:

'The *compañero* is a Christian, father. You should talk to him.'

He is a very good doctor, a very respectful man. Then I go in and there I am. Just present. I don't know what else to say. I find it too cheap to say, 'Have confidence because God...' What should I say? There are people who find it really easy to talk about God. But I just find it boring. Miguel is always able to say something about God but Miguel is profound, he is never cheap. The compas know that Miguel is always straight with them. That is why he has the right to speak about God. But I can't get the words out. I think that by temperament I prefer things to do with life and being in the thick of things.

Sadly, the *companeros* who fall in combat have to be left on the field of battle. They are buried on the spot, hurriedly, because it's nearly always necessary to retreat. I have seldom had the opportunity to bury anyone. But sometimes it happens. Then the burial is a very special event and I have the opportunity to say a few Christian words over the dead.

For example there was the burial of Herbert, a comandante. I had known him since my first day there. We buried him in the town square of Jucuarán, in Usulután. Comandante Chico 'Chicón' spoke, and several other *companeros*, and I spoke too. The people were there and the combatants. That time I said two things, there in the square:

'It's wonderful to think that when you die fighting for your people, you transcend death. That is to say you go on living, because the work for which you died goes on. Because it's not an individualistic project but a project of the people. And as the project is not dead, the dead who die for it go on living in those who go on fighting. Herbert is alive in our midst and we must go on fighting for this project. Because if we do not Herbert will die. But that's not all, that's not enough. Herbert is not only alive in this way among us. Herbert our brother, his person, his whole being, his generosity and love, what we knew of him, his whole life, is also still alive. But now he is sharing his life with God.'

That's what I said. What is life 'with God' like? We don't know, but we have that faith, that confidence, that hope. When I say this to the *companeros* it gives them hope, even to those who don't share our faith, or say they don't.

In Morazán there are some very common sayings, though they're not very Christian ones. They say, 'So-and-so conked out in the street.' It means that he died in the street, perhaps because of an accident. 'So and so conked out', even if he died from an illness. When the Day of the Dead comes round they call it the 'day of the ended'. Those who have come 'to their end'. These are two very common expressions but I don't think they are Christian ones. Not at all. For us death is not an end, it is a way through to a fuller life. We believe in a God who not only acts within history, but also acts beyond death.

I won't believe there's nothing beyond death. I believe that even more here at the front. I see these *compañeros* who are so young joining the guerrillas... And what is their whole life? Going about these muddy paths in Morazán, sleeping rough, eating hardly anything, dirty, exhausted, putting up with air raids, having to do jobs which carry a great risk... If they are lucky they last three years and then they fall in combat. And is that all there is to life? No, it can't be...

For those who have fallen in battle, the compas call out their names and say three times:

'*Presente, presente, presente!*'

Sometimes they joke about it:

'Look here, when you die we are going to shout out your *Presente...*'

And they laugh, as much as to say, 'Do you want more than that?' A comandante gets remembered that way, of course. But as for the 'compitas', the lesser *compañeros*, they get remembered for a time by those who were closest to them, but afterwards they are forgotten. There are so many dead! And what of their lives? The compitas probably had no childhood to speak of in the midst of all that poverty. And no youth. They had to live their lives with such self-sacrifice... How can such a life not find some response? That's why I refuse to believe that there's nothing beyond death.

If there is nothing, these compitas are off their heads. They're mad to risk themselves in such a way, to be so generous. Heaven is not a question of reward, it's a question of justice. Death... Archbishop Romero and Somoza were both assassinated... And now are they both the same? No, I cannot believe there will not be justice after death.

For me, God is the one who guarantees that the lives of the good will not be lost, that this compita will attain the life she or he longed for. God assures us there will be justice. I don't see that such a faith is a constraint, an alienating faith. I don't believe it, because if we can work and fight with such an optimistic vision, this encourages us rather than limiting our strength, don't you think? The compas understand all this. Sometimes during the war the danger is that we get used to death. We are going to die anyway, it's bound to happen sooner or later. That is how they think. Because in war death is always near. That's why it's important for us to be there with a Christian word of hope in the face of death.

## A just God

This attitude to death is not just important at the moment of death, it's also important in life. It puts things in perspective. There is a God to whom I am grateful, to whom I answer, a God who will do justice... My life wouldn't be the same if God didn't exist. It's not the same answering to the Party as answering to God, no... The Party, too, has limitations. Only God is the ultimate.

Sometimes people say to me at the beginning of a conversation.
'No, I don't believe in God.'

And by the end of the conversation I find they believe more than I do. I realise that these compas who tell me they don't believe in God are the ones who most frequently talk to me about God or ask me questions to make me talk. They nearly always begin with a joke, and then out pour all the problems they have with the church.

'Rogelio, we know you and you are here working with us. But what about those bishops, those priests and all those Christians who are so different from you? How do you manage to stay within that church, how can you think of yourself as part of that church?'

They have problems. And also of course, they've had lessons in marxism. And their ideas become confused. They've been told about historical materialism, so they begin to question the existence of God. In fact, though, it's not something that comes up a lot in discussion.

I think it is like when you get to a certain age and begin to reject what your parents have taught you and begin to have opinions that differ from theirs. These *compañeros* never had any Christian experience worth bothering about before. They learned to become men in the organisation. I reckon too that they learned Christian values, renunciation, self-sacrifice, sharing with others, in the organisation. They didn't learn any of this in a Christian community, because they never belonged to a community. The only thing they can remember is going to church with their granny and having to say long, boring prayers when some disaster occurred, or having to carry a stone on their heads to make it rain. In the Salvadorean countryside it's very common to see processions of people with stones on their heads. The heavier the better. The more pain, the more rain. And this is what they're rejecting when they say they don't believe in God.

They ask about God. Whether he exists or not. That's the big question. They don't ask about Jesus, because it's obvious that Jesus Christ is worth while. That's how they come to be Christians even though they say the don't believe in God. But as far as I'm concerned they are on the way to believing. Because our faith begins with Jesus Christ. I don't know if this is very theological, but it applies in my case. That's what my faith is like.

Jesus Christ, a man whose life expressed a passion for truth and justice, a man who especially loved the poor, a man able to keep going amid so many risks, so many lies and so many problems. A humble person, dedicated to a project: his determination to give his life, not to be important himself, because the only important thing was his Father. Above all, when you think about it, Jesus had faith. This makes a strong impact on me and on my faith, that Jesus too had faith. With Jesus I begin to believe.

That is why we must begin with Jesus because Jesus was a man of faith, a radical faith, who found in his relationship with God the strength to follow that road. Why discuss in philosophical terms whether the world is self-sufficient or whether there is room for God? The compas prefer the road that Jesus trod. They are already on that road. To believe in Jesus is to follow him, to follow along his road, to be like him. I tell them:

'You are Christians. Because you have his passion for truth and justice, his love for the people, the poor, his determination... Five years of war and you're still here, with your optimism, your hope. Because you have humility.'

Humility. I have to admit that it was the compas who taught me this virtue. Its one thing I don't usually have. We priests are not humble, not humble at all. We are tremendously proud. We are tremendous individualists. We always think we are important because everybody makes us feel important. I have learned from the compas the value of humility.

They wait for as long as it takes. I don't. I'm impatient, I don't like waiting. I have important things to do, I can't waste time... the compas are never impatient. They don't boast either. And they are respectful. It's always so easy to gain access to the comandantes. They are never self-important or put themselves first. They eat tortilla and beans, and they sleep on the ground. I like to watch them when they are in a group. Their main concern is 'Has everyone had something to eat?', not 'Shall we eat?'

Joaquín Villalobos is like that, so is Luisa, Comandante Luisa, so are Ana Guadalupe and Chico 'Chiquito'. They are all like that. Whether they have faith or not is another matter. But I see them as more Christian than we are, because they've given their lives totally. And that's what being Christian is about, isn't it?

One of them told me once that he admired Jesus a lot. He only had one criticism, that Jesus did not opt for violence. But I tell them that violence is not a moral problem, but primarily a political problem. And I always try to convince them that they too are not in favour of violence, that they don't want violence, but have been forced to use it in order to do away with violence once and for all. That Jesus' pacifist option was determined by a context. That even then in Jesus' time there were guerrilla groups, the Zealots, who had no chance of getting anywhere... They understand this. Jesus is never a problem. They definitely admire him.

# 5

# *Liberated zone*

## The Present Situation in the Department of Morazán

The fact that a large part of Morazán is a war-front makes it very different from other regions of the country, apart from the other war-fronts. Government repression first erupted in this area at the end of 1977, and as it grew worse many people had to leave their homes. When the war-fronts appeared in 1980 the population was panic-stricken by the bombing and strafing from the air and the persecution of everyone suspected of having links with the guerrillas. Many local people could not endure the raids, the burning down of their houses and the murders committed by the army in October 1980 and left the region. At the beginning of 1983 the army abandoned their military positions north of the River Torola. Thus the country north of this river became territory completely under guerrilla control. This situation accentuated the repressive attitude that the army subsequently adopted towards the local civilian population... In addition, the army adopted a 'scorched earth' policy in all its patrols and operations. This explains the burning of thousands and thousands of houses in the hamlets and villages.

The aim was to get rid of the population. Seizures, murders, and intimidation by bombardment and mortar attack were the most effective method to make the population flee the area. When they found that not all the people fled, they tried to isolate them by subjecting to rigid military control the transport of all food, clothing, medicine, shoes, etc. From January 1986 onwards, the military cordon regularly seized local people and confiscated their goods and in other cases drove traders out of Perquín and Torola. The situation of the approximately 20,000 inhabitants remaining is extremely delicate...

In normal circumstances Salvadorean peasants' everyday food is tortillas, eaten with a lot of salt and a few beans. After six years of war

69

and all kinds of repression and destruction of crops, it is difficult to believe that they still find anything to eat. Premature old age and the flushed faces of adults and children are the mark of a population that is being worn out...

Crops of all kinds, and especially those produced co-operatively, have been burned or destroyed...

The majority of families, whose houses are built of the usual adobe and brick, have emigrated to the cities through fear of constant bombing from the air. Their houses are occupied today by hundreds of families who have been homeless since 1980 when the armed forces went on campaign and burned every house and hut they came across...

Traditionally Salvadorean peasants buy clothes once a year and shoes as and when they can. During these six years of conflict most of the population has not even been able to buy things every two years. Most clothes are extremely worn and clothes previously regarded as worn out are being worn again. The inhabitants of the community of La Joya (Meanguera) report that some 200 people in the neighbourhood have only the clothes they stand up in and sleep out of doors where they risk being bitten by vampire bats. In the north of Morazán, the few shoes there are are worn to shreds and most of the children go barefoot. [Extract from a report drawn up by the Pastoral Team of the Eastern Communities, Morazán, July 1986.]

The 'liberated zone' stretches practically from the northern frontier to the River Torola, or a bit further, to Corinto. There are only about 20,000 inhabitants in this zone now, scattered in farms and hamlets. These are the people at whom our pastoral work is primarily aimed. We look after them. Although 'look after' is putting it too strongly. We would like to look after them. For these last few years the population has been shrinking. So many bombardments and massacres by the army have made people move away. To Honduras, to San Salvador, to the refuges. Those who have stayed and resisted are indomitable, exemplary I would say. All those years of war, and they go on sowing their beans, their maize, their rice. They have their little shops where all they sell is a little salt, a few sweets. They go by night to other villages to try and get these things. They put up their stalls, which are destroyed, and they put them up again... They keep up their vegetable gardens. If they have to go on 'manoeuvres' for a week they lose their vegetables because they can't water them. But never mind, when the 'run' is over, and the bombing slackens off, before the enemy has even left Morazán, they are out sowing again. It's a miracle how these people go on making such huge efforts every day, knowing that the enemy will destroy half their harvest. What courage! My God, what perseverance!

When I speak of 20,000 I'm referring only to Morazán. Our front extends further. San Miguel, La Unión, Usulután. There is a large civilian population there. They are all zones under more limited control, disputed territory. I work in these zones, too.

## Disputed territory

Work in zones not completely under guerrilla control is more difficult. It is a question of contacts. We hold a service in one place and then move on to another, trying to cheer the people up. In these zones I can't stay put in any one place. We also have to encourage the catechists and the delegates of the word who live there to keep up their work. I've been in Anamorós, in Esparta, in what we call 'the south', in Usulután, around Jucuarán. I've spent quite a lot of time there over these last few years. I always have the same aim: to establish contact, to encourage the delegates, and to hold services.

In these zones the FMLN has military control but the enemy is active, its propaganda is widespread, and some of the population are prejudiced against us. One thing I've discovered: if the Christians in such places have not undergone a real training but just go through the motions of religious observance, they are not strong enough to face up to these new challenges. Especially because individualist attitudes persist and they don't think in terms of the common good. That's why it's always so important to work on setting up base communities. It's the basis from which people can go on to understand what's going on and then get involved. If in our efforts to create these communities we manage to train only five people, that's still quite an achievement.

I agree that popular religion contains a core of valuable elements, but when it doesn't go on to raise people's consciousness at the same time, it's useless. I learned this from the people of Jucuarán. The people there had never belonged to a base community and had never received Christian education to enable them to understand their own history. So that made it difficult when I arrived in Jucuarán. I tried to approach the people who came to church to say the rosary. I talked to them about Mary, I said the rosary with them, even two rosaries! But as they connected me with the FMLN it was no good! And it wasn't just that, it was

71

everything. A priest who sleeps on the ground, disgraceful! Eating tortilla with his fingers, even more disgraceful! Going about all sweaty and covered in mud... They don't like it one little bit. They want a priest who sits down quietly while they wait on him. That's their image of a priest. That's what they want. The compas told me that people there were saying:

'Hmmmm, this priest has lost his dignity!'

It made me laugh. That's what they say of a girl who gets pregnant.

In Jucuarán there was a strong devotion to the Virgin of the Candelaria. When I arrived, I organised the procession of the Virgin but no one wanted to walk with me. They talked about the processions they used to have before the war, with thousands and thousands of peasants coming from miles around to pray to the Virgin who performed so many miracles. And all day long people filed through the church to give alms to the Virgin. A catechist compa who is with me now used to have to carry the sackfuls of alms to the convent. Loads of money! Now the priests who organised these processions and collected so much money have gone away. Now that the FMLN is in the area, they don't fit in, so they abandon the people and go, since it's become a dangerous place to be in...

I can't help asking myself why these priests never took advantage of these festivals, this deep religious sense, to say something worthwhile about Mary, about faith and Christian commitment. There are a lot of very interesting things to be said about Mary. All they told the people was to hurry up and drop the money in the collecting box... And one year the priest had one car and the next a new one. They said they were going to build a new church with the money, but the church is only half built and people say the priest ran off with the money. Not just the money, either: apparently he took a girl with him too... This makes me sad. There's so much corruption among some of our brother priests, such advantage taken of people's ignorance, when they could work such miracles if they built upon the people's deep religious feelings. What did they become priests for? The FMLN often laments these failings in priests, and gives us every support for another kind of work, that of creating base communities.

Nobody wanted to join in my procession. Only 20 people came, but I was determined to carry on with it. I even ordered them to form up in two columns of ten, to make it more solemn. The compas laughed about it afterwards! I went through the street with a megaphone, preaching about the Virgin Mary. Next day we held another procession. Little by little we began to get somewhere, especially with the people from the outlying hamlets. It wasn't easy work, but we did manage something. In this sort of situation I make a point of speaking out and sticking to my guns until the people say:

'Well, he isn't like the other priests we know, but we can't say he's a bad priest.'

Sometimes people are completely confused. It's largely our fault as priests, because it's our responsibility to help this deeply religious people to understand their own history. There's nothing more depressing than the sight of poor people who don't understand their own history aping the views and attitudes of the rich, in direct opposition to themselves and their own interests. Nothing is sadder.

It's not only lack of consciousness. It's also partly fear, because if the army knows they go around with Rogelio 'Poncel', they're accused of being guerrillas. It's a crime to have anything to do with me. My name is bandied about by the enemy as that of a priest who disobeys the Pope, a priest who incites people to violence. On one occasion a number of peasants in Joateca were blown up and killed by mines. The press said the mines had been laid on my orders. I don't know why they blamed it on me. They knew that I was doing pastoral work in the Joateca region, perhaps that's why.

Sometimes the army puts out rumours for the compas to hear, that they have captured me, or killed me, and that the flies are eating my corpse. They spread these lies to demoralise the compas. According to the enemy I've already died several times in Morazán.

The compas always know where I am. The person in charge of the zone knows so that he can send word for me to be met and given protection for the return journey. Sometimes they forbid me to go somewhere. It still annoys me, because we priests always like to do as we please. Afterwards I realise that the compas are right; they are doing it for my own good.

I never wear military uniform and I never carry a weapon. The catechists carry arms, but that's different. In fact I've never really run into any serious problems on the ground. Only the air raids. It would be no good my carrying arms, I'm useless at such things. I can't even use a pistol. For me, going around unarmed also symbolises how important it is to remember that violence is not ideal. Violence is a painful necessity, but what we want is peace. The *compañeros* understand this. They don't think of a priest as an armed man. At least that's what I've found. I think I have better access to the civilian population if I'm unarmed, although they quite understand that for my protection I go around with people who do carry arms. No-one's worried by that.

I've been criticised by the regime and by some priests. How can a priest go about with armed men? But the day the Pope came to San Salvador I could see that he was surrounded by armed men, and not just a few humble compitas with a little pistol each, but by well-trained and well-armed guards. So what about that?

### Something to celebrate

Our people in arms, our people are advancing throughout the entire country. As we have reported, the Farabundo Martí National Liberation Front occupied the town of Corinto last Sunday, after heavy fighting with the enemy. Radio Venceremos will now transmit a recording made in the streets of Corinto, Morazán, sent to us by our mobile broadcasting unit in the area:

Radio Venceremos, the official voice of the Farabundo Martí National Liberation Front, reporting from the front line of the 'Francisco Sánchez' Eastern Front in the town of Corinto.

Today, 3 February 1982, the year of the people's victories, the FMLN forces have Corinto, in the Department of Morazán, under their political and military control.

After a devastating advance by our army and people, jointly with the forces of our people's militias and health brigades, and with the co-operation of the local inhabitants, the FMLN revolutionary army has taken control of Corinto and the surrounding area.

On 31 January the forces of our revolutionary army advanced in three directions, north, south and west. That same day our forces reduced to six the number of the enemy's positions in the town of Corinto. A group of National Guards and paramilitaries retreated to the National Guard Barracks, a second group took refuge in the tower of Corinto church, and another in a strategic position, a strongly fortified two-storey house.

During the night our revolutionary forces, with the help of the people of Corinto and our popular militias, lit bonfires on every street corner to make it easier for our combatants to see what they were doing.

On 1 February, our forces continued to advance, driving the enemy back to a single position by the end of the day, the church tower of

Corinto. The same day our people's army gained total military control of this district in the department of Morazán [Radio Venceremos broadcast, 3 February 1982].

It's a really happy occasion when I arrive to celebrate mass after the *compañeros* have taken a town. I've been present on several such occasions: Corinto, Anamorós, Chirilagua... I'm not involved in the fighting, but I arrive afterwards, when the town has been taken. It's difficult to describe how happy we feel.

It's so difficult, living rough as we do. To arrive suddenly in a little town is like reaching heaven. With people, shops, people walking about. With electric light! People's first reaction is always very positive. After enduring the tense moments of the siege, with shots flying around, having to lie flat on the ground for hours, all that fear... When it's all over and our army enters the town, it's a moment of real happiness. I invite them to celebrate the eucharist and they come. I explain what has happened from a Christian point of view and I encourage them. The *compañeros* walk about as pleased as can be, swigging cold drinks, and they often organise a dance with Los Torogoces. The girls love to dance with a guerrilla, although most of the compas can't dance very well! They play country dances, *rancheras* and *cumbias* and everyone has a wonderful time.

After the joy comes the fear, because when we take the town the army goes away, but after a day or two they nearly always try to take it back, and the fighting begins again. The bombing frightens the people. This permanent state of war demoralises them. Who isn't afraid of war?

Many people have left, which is why fewer children are born and there aren't as many baptisms as there were at the beginning. But there are still some. The christening ceremony is very simple. We always perform it during a mass. I'm very insistent that being baptised is not just a social occasion. I tell them that in Zacamil a baptism was nearly always an excuse for a blow-out with music playing full blast for dancing, and the father, godfather and uncle knocking back the booze in a back-room before the ceremony. Here at the front there's always cold drink of some kind made from fruit, mango or whatever's available. That's what a feast amounts to here: cold fruit drink. There's no problem getting fruit. The problem is sugar.

I also reassure the parents, the godparents and the whole community that we are not baptising the child for fear it might go to purgatory or to hell. They sometimes feel this fear, because they have been taught to be afraid.

'No, brothers and sisters, God cannot be so cruel as to condemn this child, who is so innocent and so lovely. We do not baptise from fear but out of commitment, to commit ourselves, because you want this child to belong to the Christian community. I ask the parents, the godparents and this community, are you truly willing to educate this little one, to awaken its consciousness, so that it will grow up to be a man or woman who is willing to fight for their country?'

They often give children the names of an older son or daughter or some other member of the family who has been killed in battle. Many are called Oscar, or Arnulfo after Archbishop Romero, and Octavio after Father Octavio Ortiz. I always tell the community everyone must come and kiss the baby to congratulate it. Peasants are shy, so sometimes they hesitate. We always end with a big round of applause to mark a new addition to our family. It's a very happy occasion.

## Confession

We don't administer the sacrament of confession very much. Really I didn't want to encourage traditional confessions. I could easily say: 'Queue here for confession!', and up they would come to form a long queue, just because it's the custom. The peasants usually come to the priest to confess to giving someone an evil look, using bad language, little things like that... But I want to avoid this. Since I don't take the initiative to set up this kind of confession, they don't ask for it. At the beginning of mass I always say, 'Let us make an act of contrition together. Let us recognise our limitations. Everyone can come forward to receive communion, without any qualms.'

What happens sometimes is that I have a chat with a compa, and he will lament his lack of commitment, his moral failings, things that affect his commitment to the people. Some also discuss violence with me, because they have had to kill, or they have had to execute someone.

'Father, what do you say about that?'

I consider these talks, which sometimes last a long time, to be confessions. At the end I say:

'Brother, this has been a confession, because you've spoken me with great humility and sincerity and we've cleared up a good many things. So I think God has been present in this talk with his forgiveness, his mercy and love, to raise us up and to direct us on a more perfect way. So if you like, if you want, I can give you absolution.'

'Oh, was that a confession?'

They remember what they have always understood by 'confession' — kneeling in the confessional — and they are surprised. I'm not saying this sort of thing happens every day. But when it does I'm really pleased, and they are too.

The compas also have sessions of what they call criticism and self-criticism. The local people do it too, in quite a disciplined way. These meetings are also really a form of confession. And there is greater sincerity and honesty than in the confessional. What's more, the whole community is present and taking part. Each person in turn makes a self-criticism and when he or she has finished, the others have the right to criticise and say, you left out this, we've noticed that, what you are doing here is not revolutionary. Each person makes a self-criticism and receives criticism from all the others. It is done with warmth and great frankness. I take part too. I feel sorry that they don't criticise me much, although they've gradually begun do it more. They don't like it when I get angry, or when I'm nervy or impatient. They think it's worse for a priest to get angry than to have a woman. They don't expect us to get angry, and they criticise me when I do, especially of late. At the beginning they kept quiet and laughed. It means a lot to them to have a priest with them and they feel shy of criticising me. These meetings are good. We priests are trained to hide our defects and to air them like this in front of everybody is hard for us.

In these meetings for criticism and self-criticism there's a good deal of discussion. Some find it hard to accept criticism. But at the end of the day they are always left in peace. The criticisms are made with a lot of respect. I think they're a confession. Especially as they are in front of the community. I think perhaps this is why there's no need for the compas to go to confession with me. So these occasions are very valuable, don't you think?

## El Mozote

I've always found it hard to understand executions. But the compas must have a different point of view. On one occasion a *compañero* asked to talk to me:

77

'Well, come at one o'clock on Thursday.'

'Oh no, I can't come then because at one o'clock I've got an execution.' 'So what time can you come?'

'At half past one, when I've finished.'

He arrived at one-thirty, perfectly calm. After an execution... Of an informer, a case that had been thoroughly investigated. The people they execute are those who have given away whole families, families who've been assassinated because they were fingered by the informer. What should be done with these people?

'Father, this is a job. I have to do it. How can we let a man go free who is killing others?'

Then we moved on to talk about other things. The organisation takes great care to make sure the compas don't get obsessed with executions. They are very careful about it. I think it's a good thing to be scrupulous about violence. And the compas try to keep it up. I like hearing Joaquín Villalobos. He always insists that our task is not to destroy, much less to kill. And if a compa steps out of line on this point, they call him in for a reprimand, or even punish him.

Sometimes they execute a *compañero* who has turned traitor. I always insist they investigate very carefully, that execution should be the last resort, because we are not the owners of other people's lives. It is important to keep this perspective, because if a man thinks he is the owner of life where will he stop? I think of Marcial and Ana María.* Marcial had a great record as a revolutionary, but he went off the rails. He thought he was God! When someone thinks he is God he no longer values life. He killed Ana María and in an exceptionally cruel way. It's important, even in politics, that God should always remain the only owner of lives.

One day they told me about a *compañero* who had to be executed. The *compañero* asked a favour before they shot him:

'I should like to say a few words.'

'All right. Say them.'

'I understand that I have to die and I agree I deserve it. But I'm sorry for what I've done.'

---

*'Marcial', Salvador Cayetano Carpio, was the celebrated leader of the FPL, the FMLN guerrilla group which established a 'liberated zone' in Chalatenango, in the north of El Salvador, at the same time as the ERP established its zone in Morazán. In 1983 internal strife within the FPL leadership led to the brutal murder in Nicaragua of 'Ana María', the FPL second-in-command, by another member of the group. Marcial was held responsible, and shortly afterwards committed suicide.

Then he took off his shoes.

'I leave my shoes here to be given to a *compañero*. Let him not use them to go the way I went, but keep instead to the straight and narrow...'

The *compañeros* who had to shoot him hesitated. But the order had already been given and it's a military matter. They shot him. Apparently when they told the comandantes their eyes filled with tears.

They execute people, certainly, but they are not brutal or heartless. We must always be scrupulous about violence, because that is healthy. But we mustn't pretend that war isn't war. War is war. I'm always pleased when they say there have been enemy casualties. No, I've never seen the enemy dead, never. They don't let me go into the firing line.

When they killed Colonel Monterrosa I was really glad. I was very near the place where this operation happened. I can't tell you the whole story of how the compas did it. One day it will be told, it's an incredible story... But how delighted we were when we found out that the trap they had set for this man had been successful, because he was responsible for the massacre in El Mozote and he was killed very near where he had murdered so many people.

In La Joya, very near the place where Monterrosa was killed, there was a celebration of the word with the community, to give thanks to God. The theme of the service was God does justice through his people. And there were games and dancing. We were so happy about what had happened! Some Europeans are scandalised when I tell them this, it really worries them that we are glad about Monterrosa's death. They don't realise what this means for the people. They don't realise that it's not just a question of the death of one person, but of the deaths that person has caused and might have gone on causing. We are not rejoicing about someone's tragic death, nor do we make a final judgment on it. That's not for us to do, but what we saw in that death was how God rejects evil and never abandons his people. That's why we were glad.

Monterrosa was a murderer. He ordered the massacre in El Mozote in December 1981. I was on the run when this happened. It was a tremendous shock to me. I had been so often to this village... It had quite a large population and little shops. In El Mozote you could even have a Coca-Cola! And when you come in from the hills after being there for two months solid, a cold fizzy drink is like a dream... I often went there and said mass there many times. And my message was always of hope; that what is happening, what we are experiencing is not the end, that we are on our way to better times; that God is not indifferent to so much suffering; he is very close to us, a God who plays a direct role in our history. I always spoke like that. The people came to the service, and we prayed and sang with Los Torogoces. It was lovely to go to El Mozote.

That's the place where it happened. The army came. The people there had never gone on the run; they were too trusting. It's no easy thing to go on the run anyway. They were warned to go, but they refused; they didn't want to abandon their homes, their fields. They were convinced God wouldn't let anything happen to them. And the troops arrived and killed more than 1000 peasants. They accused them of being guerrillas. Their policy during those years was to exterminate the potential social base for the guerrillas as rapidly as possible. They killed *en masse*. Nowadays they're still trying to do the same thing, but they no longer kill in this way. They try to win over the people by giving or withholding food. Of course, it's the same old army and the people have seen so much cruelty that they're scarcely about to fall for that one...

More than 1000 peasants murdered. I'm not exaggerating. I saw many of the mutilated corpses rotting. For days afterwards there was an unbearable smell. The houses destroyed, everyone dead... In that village which for me had meant so much happiness, the women and children, children we never see now playing on the hills... El Mozote was such a happy place, with so much life in it... When I saw the piles of dead bodies, the destruction, I couldn't bear it. How is it possible that just here where I have come so many times to say that God is a God who is close to us and who loves us, who is not indifferent to suffering, that in this very place there should be such a horrendous massacre? At these moments I wonder what I'm doing, what on earth I'm talking about... Perhaps I should be doing something else. I'll take up a gun and they can kill me in the first battle. I'm not going to go on talking, what's the point of it?

So many people I knew were killed. Good people who lived there, innocent people, my friends... I remember the sacristan of the chapel, such a pleasant man. He always used to ask me:

'Father, is this war going to end soon?'

'It won't be long.'

They killed him. Words fail me to describe what they did. My faith is very fragile.

While the President, José Napoleón Duarte, manipulated the story of the Nativity in his New Year speech and called for peace, reconciliation and for popular confidence in his government, in the villages of Cerro Pando, Poza Honda, La Joya and El Mozote in the department of Morazán, more than a thousand peasants were brutally massacred by the army in an act of indescribable cruelty. To add insult to injury and in flagrant disregard for all that is sacred, in the village of El Mozote the church itself, where we had celebrated the word and presence of God, was chosen as the place to round up the men of the village and shoot them, men who were the children of God the Father and temples of the Holy Spirit. Moreover certain objects kept for the celebration of mass were abused, thrown away and trampled. Afterwards part of the church itself was destroyed. Its ruins now cover the corpses of countless brothers, victims of this horrendous crime.

In the villages of Cerro Pando and Poza Honda, most of the victims were members of evangelical communities, highly respected for their religious fervour and practice of Christian brotherhood, as taught us in the holy scriptures. For this reason, the massacre also has the character of sacrilege. That is to say, it is a terrible offence against God, and Christian consciences cannot remain indifferent to it. Therefore we appeal to the Catholic parish communities of El Salvador, the continent and the world and the evangelical communities within and beyond our frontiers to dedicate their main service or mass on Sunday 10 January as a requiem for those who were killed and as an act of atonement for the sacrilege committed in the church of El Mozote. Wherever possible there should be joint ecumenical services to mark the sorrow that has engulfed our people.

We propose that the service should have the following three aims:

1. To denounce the crimes and give details of the tragic events, described in full by Radio Venceremos, and to lay the blame on the military high command, the Christian Democrat military junta and imperialism, whose vile action was not accidental but in accordance with a coldly premeditated plan.
2. To raise awareness of the need to organise and redouble our solidarity efforts. This is the only way our people can be defended against a premeditated plan of extermination. This defence is not just a right but a duty because our lives do not belong to us and we therefore have a duty to take care of them and use appropriate means to do so.

81

3. To come together in our communities to beseech God to put an end to so much suffering and let justice triumph over oppression, good over evil and love over hate.

We invite you all to join in on Sunday 10 January in memory of the thousand peasants killed and to make atonement for the acts of sacrilege committed in the department of Morazán [Message of Father Rogelio Ponseele to the Salvadorean people and to the world, broadcast by Radio Venceremos on 5 January 1982].

Monterrosa gave the order for the crime in El Mozote; he was in charge. God brought him to justice. Before the El Mozote massacre, there had been another massacre in El Junquillo. I saw the people fleeing and coming to the village where I was at the time. That was horrible too. They destroyed one man's house and killed all his family. He had nothing. That night I gave him my blanket. People fleeing try to save something, a pot to cook with, something, anything. That man had nothing, he lost everything.

Later, the compas captured Captain Medina Garay, who was responsible for that massacre. He always kept up a stance of arrogance. Many compas in the camp wanted to see justice done, to have him executed, because Medina had killed their little brothers and sisters or their parents. He was really an evil man. After a while he escaped. They captured him again. In the end they exchanged him for some *compañeros* who had been taken prisoner. It was very difficult for the command to convince the *compañeros*. They wanted to kill him and were not happy that he was exchanged.

FMLN policy has always been one of respect for prisoners, even with officers like these. Medina himself was wounded and he was given medical care. They treated him like any other prisoner of war. What will we do in El Salvador in the hour of our triumph with the military who've been responsible for the repression? Will we forgive them, as they did in Nicaragua? At the moment, the attitude I see is one of great respect. It's not just propaganda when the compas say they comply with the international conventions. They really do comply with them. It's a matter of honour, because they are not destroyers, they are not murderers. Sadly they have had to resort to violent means, but their aim is to build a new country, not to destroy. When victory comes, what they do with these murderers will be decided on political grounds. These matters have to be considered not just on Christian criteria.

We have to submit our Christian judgment to a political analysis in these delicate matters.

I think forgiveness is a Christian contribution. But even the *compañeros* who are not Christian are capable of forgiving. The compas don't hate. This can be seen when they capture soldiers. Ordinary rank and file soldiers. You won't believe me, but after about half an hour the compas already consider them *compañeros*. Sometimes they are chatting away with them and they haven't even disarmed them. If they are hungry they give them food and tend their wounds. There are exceptions, but normally what we see every day is that people here have an enormous ability to convert moral pain not into hatred, but into strength to continue the struggle. The guerrillas always stress that the soldiers in the army belong to the people and we are fighting for them too, that we have the same interests, that they are just mistaken.

I have stayed and talked to these soldier prisoners. In the end they recognise that they are mistaken and they realise that what they have been told about the guerrillas isn't true. Some join the FMLN, others leave the country. But even those who leave do so with very different ideas from those they had at first. They have not found hatred, they have been forgiven, not just with words but with deeds.

### The children
The children are affected by the war. They live with it. Their games are war games. With a piece of wood for a gun they lay ambushes... In a more severe air raid they get frightened of course, and they cry when they have to stay in a shelter for many hours, in hiding from the bombs.

When they grow up a bit they are quick-witted, astute, with a very adult mentality. At ten they are already adults. They talk about the war and make 'analyses'. At twelve they are already running errands. They carry messages, for example. They know how to find their way through the midst of the enemy and they get the job done. Not long afterwards they are actually fighting!

They are children who never had a childhood, but they are not bad, they are not tainted by violence. It is as though they understand why this war is going on and that they have their own role to play in it. This isn't hatred; in my book, it's dignity. They are defending their families, defending their country. And if you ask them why they are fighting they'll give you a complete lecture. They learn from their own experience:

'They killed my mother.'

'My brother is with the guerrillas.'

And at school we make them discuss what their lives were like:

'What did you eat at home?'

'Just beans.'

'Did you drink milk?'

'There wasn't any.'

They learn quickly. Increasingly they are sending the smallest ones to refuges in the capital with their mothers. These continual invasions by the army frighten them a lot. They take their toll. The ones who are a bit older stay behind. You can see them running about barefoot in all the stones and mud. And they survive.

I remember one. What was he called? What was it? I forget the names. It's because in the front we don't say names, just 'compa'. And what's more we're always substituting pseudonyms for our real names. Ah yes, he was called Chío. He was quite small when I went to bring him to Pueblo Viejo, near Gotera, so that he could study in a little school in Morazán. I walked seven hours with him. It was a very tough journey for the boy and he cried. He had seen the soldiers kill his mother in a massacre. They had also killed two of his brothers and all his other brothers and sisters were members of the organisation. He wanted to join up too, and fight. He was eight years old.

He started going to school, and he was a good student. Later he learned more and worked in radio. Now he is a proper compa, in the communications section, because he learned to read and write really well. The children I saw when I arrived here are all guerrillas now. Time has passed... With the children of Morazán we often sing 'Quincho Barrilete', the song from Nicaragua. They like this song a lot, because Quincho is like them: a child with dignity who goes out to fight for his people.

## Camp life

We carry on pastoral work with the civilian population as well as with the guerrillas, but we live with the guerrillas in the camps. They don't want us to stay with the civilians for security reasons, in case the enemy springs a surprise and creates problems. If we get caught for the night somewhere, we send word ahead that we're going to stay there. But normally we look for the nearest camp. We don't have any camp which is our own fixed one. We live in any of the camps with the compas.

At the war front you have to get up very early and always be prepared. When dawn breaks, it's still rather dark. It's about half past four, or a quarter to five... We begin the day by singing the *Internationale* — 'Arise ye starvelings from your slumbers!' Then we sing the national anthem. But no-one's up to singing much at that hour of morning, and the compas are always way out of tune. Each one comes in when he feels like it, some very high, others very low, and he who sings loudest sets the key. I've tried to explain that they should start off together and in the same key. But it's no use, they don't understand. It sounds awful.

Then comes the morning work-out: half an hour's jogging, then exercises. I like this way of beginning the day. Now I can run as well and keep up with them. At the beginning I always lagged behind. They could all run faster than me. I arrived in Morazán weighing 15 stone 10lbs. A well-fed priest! I hadn't done any sport for years. Now I weigh 11 stone 6lbs. I left all my fat behind on these hills. And it went quickly! I feel better for it, though; it's a very healthy life.

Because food is scarce and we do all that walking, it keeps our weight down. Even when there are no 'manoeuvres', I sometimes have to walk for four hours to reach a community. For the first three months my stomach was upset because of the change. But since then I haven't had flu once, no catarrh or headaches. Here the most common illness is malaria because of the mosquitoes. Apart from that the compañeros are very seldom ill. It's a very healthy environment. The sunlight is very strong — you get really burnt! And the rains are heavy — you get soaked by one storm after another. And you get tired, really exhausted. It's a physically demanding life.

The guerrillas smoke, it's true. Cigarettes mean a lot to them. The leaders always make sure there are enough to go round. Once I asked why they made such a thing about smoking, why they were so bothered about it. I don't smoke, by the way. They explained how important it is for a smoker to have a cigarette when he goes into combat. For the nerves.

Drink no. Alcohol is completely forbidden. Even at festivals there's not a drop of liquor. They make no compromises whatsoever on this point. You cannot allow it when people are carrying weapons. Once a Mexican journalist arrived on 25

December and he brought bottles and bottles of rum, hoping to please us. He thought of inviting the comandantes and drinking a toast with them on Christmas Day. But they didn't touch a drop. There's none for Christmas Eve nor for New Year's Eve, nor for any other occasion. They are absolutely rigid about that.

After jogging we go to bathe in the river, all together, everyone naked of course. There's no problem about this. I found it hard at the beginning. You get accustomed to having a house with a bathroom and going in and shutting the door, and then when you've locked the door you get undressed.

Here I had to bathe in the midst of all the *compañeros*, men and women. It was a new experience for me, but it's perfectly natural. Perhaps you're more hung up about it, if you have a petit bourgeois background. For them it's the most natural thing in the world. I've never seen any of the men make an indecent gesture towards the women.

After we've bathed, we're ready to begin the day. Breakfast comes: two tortillas, a few beans. A little coffee sometimes, but not always. Sometimes there's real coffee. In Perquín there is. Mostly we have maize coffee. For me, as long as it's coffee-coloured and hot, it's delicious.

After breakfast we meet with the catechists who are there, say a prayer, meditate together, say an Our Father, sing a hymn and then begin planning what we're going to do during the day, who will go to which community, who will come with me, who will go elsewhere, how long it will take, etc. And off we go, walking, three or four hours to reach the communities.

Everyone does their own washing, though not every day. Sometimes with soap, sometimes there isn't any. We wash on a stone by a stream. If a *compañera* wants to cheer me up me she may offer:

'Shall I wash it?'

But usually I don't accept. Because they have their own clothes to wash and their jobs to do.

'No, I have more time than you. And anyway I've got to learn.'

How hard I find it, learning! These trousers are so hard! And washing on a stone bent double. And how difficult jeans are to rinse. It's almost impossible to get rid of the soap... I think we men have less strength to wash clothes than women. They get the soap out easily with great skill. Washing isn't a task a priest is really used to. One day there were some German journalists there and I began washing, it was my day. And they rushed for their cameras! Hot news: a priest washing his own trousers!

In the camp there are very few wristwatches. For sentry duty they always use mine. Each person has to stand watch at night for an hour or an hour and a half. Often it's for the sake of discipline more than because of the danger of the enemy nearby. Whenever I arrive in camp I always put myself on the list for guard duty. It's the only time when I stand with a weapon in my hand, watching the moon, if there is one.

The compas are always asking:

'Father, lend me your watch for guard duty.'

I'm a bit afraid of lending it because they always ruin the strap. They're always trying to undo it at the wrong place. And they change the time so that they don't have to be on guard so long.

For military work the compas have watches and use them. But apart from that, time here is of no importance. They say:

'Meeting tomorrow at eight in such and such a place!'

And I'm there at five minutes to eight. I can't be late, I find it very difficult to be late. Someone goes by:

'Rogelio you're early. What's happened?

'Didn't you say eight o'clock?'

'Yes, but go and have a rest, we won't be beginning till later.'

And these are meetings with the military leaders! The war keeps time but nothing else does. And it's even worse with the local population. One day they asked me:

'Father can we have a mass for a fallen *compañero* on Monday?'

'Certainly, with pleasure. At what time would you like it?'

'No, Father, you have a lot to do, you say the time.'

That was at the beginning. I thought, if I celebrate at eight by half past nine I will be free and can do other things. I told them eight o'clock.

'Fine, Father. At eight then.'

And I hurried to be there by eight. But the mass didn't start till eleven. They get up very early, make tortillas, grind maize, clean the house a bit, do the washing. And when all this routine has been got through they begin to think:

'There's a mass; we must get ready.'

Time doesn't worry them at all. Gustavo Gutiérrez says that for Latin people clocks and diaries are an aggression. I'm beginning to understand the truth of this!

# The radio

Exactly on the hour Radio Venceremos goes on the air. It is an underground radio, literally. It has to be to survive. At least 50 people work for the radio, a whole team. The announcers, the editors, those monitoring broadcasts from San Salvador and abroad, the librarians, the security workers. The recording studio, the generators, the equipment, everything is carefully looked after, underground. When there is an invasion or a landing and it is near Radio Venceremos, they have to take the radio on manoeuvres, like the wounded. And there is a well-organised evacuation team to take out all the equipment, the microphones, recorders, and all the fragile equipment that has to be carefully looked after. The archives, the papers... when the moment comes to evacuate, each person knows what they have to carry in their pack, this microphone, that piece of paper. In ten minutes everything is out and the radio can go on manoeuvres.

As soon as it's time to go on the air and we're sure that we're out of danger, the person carrying the aerial runs to the nearest hill and starts setting up the electrical equipment. They unpack various bits and pieces, and somehow, I don't know how, exactly on the hour: 'Radio Venceremos! The official voice of the Farabundo Martí National Liberation Front!' As if nothing had happened. It's always like this wherever they are. Sometimes in the middle of a run — wham! They stop and begin broadcasting. How do they do it? I don't understand the first thing about radio but those who do say that this is amazing.

Santiago has always been one of the main voices on the radio. He arrived in Morazán at the same time as I did. He never gets a sore throat, despite the fact that they speak so loudly on the radio, as if they had the entire population in front of them. They wave their arms and get all worked up. Santiago has always been up there, never tiring. He has never left Morazán and never heard the radio from outside. When anyone comes from outside he always asks:

'How does it sound? Is it easy to pick up?'

What do they say about the radio, outside? That's what he's interested in. He's in love with the radio.

'Mariposa' is the girl who most often speaks with him on Venceremos. She too has a tremendous voice. Sometimes we have an outdoor political meeting, and from 300 yards away she shouts 'Rrrrevolution or Death!'. She has an amazingly powerful voice.

How come that through all these years the enemy has never been able to track down the radio and silence it? Everyone wonders. With all the sophisticated equipment the gringos have, they still can't do it. This makes the compas very proud.

I speak on Radio Venceremos. I've been doing it regularly ever since I arrived, since the period just before the general offensive in 1981. At that time I spoke to encourage people to join the insurrection. I said the time had come when we should assume our responsibility as Christians, and since all other roads had been closed to us, it was now a question of fighting and fighting with a gun in our hands.

I often go and record a broadcast because we frequently pass close to the radio. I prefer it that way, to speak on the spot. At other times I give a talk and record it and send it with a compa. There are always special programmes at Christmas, during Holy Week, and for some festivals and anniversaries. On Saturday and Sunday we always have reflections on the gospel. In many places when I arrive for the first time the people already know me through Venceremos.

'Ah, you are Poncel? We've heard you on the radio...' Santiago has never been able to pronounce my name the way it sounds in Flemish. So Ponseele became Poncel and this is the name that has stuck. I think that speaking on the radio is a great opportunity for us to preach the gospel. People are really impressed to hear a priest speaking on the FMLN radio. And they listen to what we say, it interests them.

The Ash Wednesday liturgy, with which Lent begins, was celebrated in all our communities. For our people Lent doesn't begin on Ash Wednesday or end on Holy Saturday. For them Lent is a permanent state of affairs. That is to say that every day our people practise that fasting which is pleasing to God, which according to the prophet Isaiah consists in breaking the chains, undoing the shackles, setting free the oppressed, breaking down every kind of slavery, sharing bread with the hungry, sheltering the homeless, clothing the naked and never turning our backs on our brothers or sisters. In the liturgical sense, Lent for our people is a time for deeper reflection and for arriving at decisions. Everything the liturgy says during Lent and Holy Week helps them reinforce their morale for the daily confrontation with an enemy who is becoming ever more cruel.

Our recent experience in the Joateca zone, during the 'Torola V' operation, was tremendously painful. In all the communities the army robbed and destroyed crops, captured many people, searched houses in the most brutal way, assaulted some villagers and tortured others. One of their victims was Mercedes Gutiérrez, an old lady from Estancias, in Cacaopera district. As a result of the torture inflicted on her she has become a virtual invalid. They murdered several people, including Jeremías Márquez and Anastasio Pereira, whose bodies were found with their throats slit. Then they engaged in indiscriminate revenge bombings, mortar and machine-gun attacks, and when they left they threatened to come back and punish anyone who listened to the FMLN. This included punishing anyone taking part in religious services conducted by our pastoral team because, the colonel said, 'that priest is contrary'.

For once he was right. I am contrary. And all of us who make up the base communities and all of us who are part of this just and honest people, are contrary to this project of terror and death. The brutal and criminal actions of the army against the civilian population have no justification whatever, because the people have every right to live in a zone under the control of the FMLN, they have every right to listen those who are at present looking after their immediate needs and they have every right to take part in religious services organised by our pastoral team.

During Lent and Holy Week our Christian people will be spending their time reflecting, nourishing their faith on God's word, a word which favours the poor, like that which Jesus addressed to the oppressed, to those who suffer, the humble and the meek: 'Blessed are the poor among you, those who trust in God and are open to the fulfilment of his will that all should have life. Yours is the kingdom. Blessed are those of you who mourn because you see the opposition there is to the building of the kingdom, and because you see the injustice and ambition of those who prevent the creation of a better world. You shall be comforted. Blessed are those of you who hunger and thirst for justice, that is, who want a new society to arise, the product of love and justice. You shall be satisfied. And blessed are those who are persecuted for my sake for trying to bring about God's plan. This will get you into trouble and you will be slandered, maligned and persecuted, but the kingdom belongs to you.'

Brothers and sisters, the future belongs to the poor because neither North American imperialism, nor Duarte, and certainly not the colonel, shall have the last word. God has the last word and that word is a word of truth and justice [Meditation by Father Rogelio Ponseele broadcast on Radio Venceremos, 23 February 1985].

# 6

# *Faith and revolution*

The *compañeros* have a great respect for the people's faith. They have great respect for what we preach. They like this image of a God who takes sides with the poor, a God who is more powerful than Reagan and the armed forces, a God who is close to us, to the little people, to the humble, and who gives us strength and offers us a challenge, a commitment.

They have great respect for the pastoral work that we do. They know the importance of the pastoral work that was done all over El Salvador before the war began, and they can see how much it raised the consciousness of the people and what a difference that has made now, in such a long struggle. Miguel, for example who before the war worked so hard here in Morazán. He opened the way among this deeply religious people. And from then on they began organising themselves for the struggle. The same thing happened all over El Salvador, during these years. We were laying the foundations. The FMLN knows this and appreciates it. This work of sowing the seed is not, as some call it, 'instrumentalisation', and the people don't just treat it as a tactic. It's a question of being objective about the reality of El Salvador today, because this is a deeply religious people.

Joaquín Villalobos once told me that they are absolutely convinced that the gospel — he didn't say the church — is the best way of motivating Salvadoreans to work for human fulfilment. Literally, that's what he said. He also said perhaps some time in the next fifty years we could have a seminar in a university to discuss religion, the idealist and the materialist views of the world, but that until then we would never quarrel about these matters. I believe him. Sometimes people tell me I'm very naive, that they're manipulating me, that they're using me now and will discard me later. But I see their everyday conduct. And I know they would never do that. Their leadership consists of men and women of great moral quality.

There's no problem with the leaders. With some of the middle-rankers in the organisation what happens is that they begin to study a little Marxism and then they say:

'Well, it seems that Marx didn't believe in God...'

Or they notice one of their leaders who doesn't believe in God either. You have to understand, these are leaders who march alongside them, take risks with them, are in the line of fire with them, who eat the same beans with them or don't eat so that they can eat... and they don't believe in God. That puts them in a quandary, because for a peasant being good is the same thing as believing in God.

'So how come that such a good and dedicated person does not believe in God?'

'Marx is the one who had the very best ideas about how to change this mess. And he didn't believe in God...'

These are very challenging questions for them. Hence some of them reject their faith. You can understand it.

The church always puzzles them. When the Pope came to El Salvador, there was hope, even among the leaders, that he might say something clear in support of the people's just struggle. The message he had sent before his visit seemed quite good to us, as it spoke about dialogue... There was hope, and among the people a good deal of hope. They imagined the Pope would come and then suddenly, just like that, there would be peace. The people feel a kind of adoration for the Pope.

He came and the people didn't understand much of what he said. That's the truth. The compas were very sad and disillusioned. They got over it quickly enough, because it's clear to them that the Pope, the bishops, the church, are a political institution that operates within the correlation of political forces like any other power. And they know they have to treat the church like that, like a world power. They have to analyse its movements and engage in all the necessary political manoeuvres to deal with it. The leaders know perfectly well how to distinguish between this power with which they have to manoeuvre and the church of the base communities. They understand the difference very well.

I've never felt for a moment that I was being manipulated. You might think that I was if you confuse these *compañeros* with the leaders of political parties, the traditional parties, who make a speech here and put on a cloth cap when they're going to speak to workers, and then off to make another speech somewhere else and in the evening they eat very well and sleep tight... No, these men are different. They are really committed. And I watch them in action from morning till night.

When we have a meeting with them, the relation established between us is important. We do our church work as church work but we have to co-ordinate with them. I'm always very anxious to hear the current political guidelines so that our pastoral work can advance and be co-ordinated. And they're equally anxious to hear from us what the mood is in the civilian population, what criticisms they are making and what they are worried about. They want to know how the communities are growing and consolidating, and how this social force of really committed people is getting stronger. They're always open and interested in that.

Sometimes they're busy making grand plans in terms of the war and their wider political objectives and they forget to take account of the lesser, more specific needs of the population: that so-and-so has a field sown here and can't abandon it, that he's got his little house, that if the husbands are sent off to do a particular job the women will be left alone... For every step careful preparation is needed, and a lot of patience. Things that affect people in this way can't just be decided over people's heads, on the basis of orders from above... We challenge them when this happens. And they're always very willing to listen to such criticisms and to hear what's being said to us when we go round the communities.

Our position towards the FMLN is one of independence and co-ordination. We make decisions about the civilian population in dialogue, together. They have the right to decide how the war must be carried on, that's their province. But decisions about the life of the communities are for the church to make. It's up to them, though, to give us a political report. The *compañeros* have much greater political clarity. They have the training and the information.

This matter of independence and co-ordination is clear enough, but questions arise. They're also very conscious of being the vanguard of the people, and they really are. They are leading the people in their struggle, they are its vanguard. Since they understand that faith is part of the people's consciousness, they have a tendency also to want to lead the people's faith.

What's happening is that a church is being born here which no longer lives for itself, but which expresses the faith of the people. That's why new questions continually crop up among us, and that's why we need to know each other, co-ordinate our work and support each other.

## No privacy

In these meetings there are always interruptions. Couriers arrive, a slip of paper with a message, that the enemy is here, that they have moved somewhere else, news of a bombing in some place, that those who are deploying in a particular direction are having a rough time, that there were casualties here, that an operation failed there, that there are supply problems... It's difficult directing a war, very difficult. I would be dead by now, not from a bomb or bullet, just from thinking about the responsibility.

The leaders stay awake day and night. Joaquín Villalobos never sleeps. He's a very humble man, of great moral quality. They are tireless. He meets with the comandantes, for a whole day of planning, discussing and thinking how to do things. And suddenly:

'Bring on Los Torogoces! And tell Supplies to get us a couple of chickens and we'll have a party!'

They're always anxious the *compañeros* should have a party of some kind from time to time to help them stand the strain of such a tense situation. Little things like that are important, aren't they? He himself leads a very austere life. Sometimes in Europe they say that Joaquín is the warmonger, the hard man, the monster! Yet he's a man obsessed with peace and dialogue. I live with them, I know them.

The compas like me chatting to them and they like chatting to me. I'm still very much a European in things like this, though. If I've got a plan of work, I find it difficult to depart from it. At the end of the day I always want to have got through 'my agenda'. How absurd this is, totally absurd, in wartime! But now I'm making a confession to you aren't I? I accuse myself of not being sociable enough and sometimes I try to avoid these long conversations. They always begin in the same way.

'Rogelio, where are you off to?'

'I have to do so and so.'

'No, Rogelio, sit down, sit down with us and tell us a yarn...'

For the peasants 'the yarn' is of key importance. It's telling a story. They don't entertain themselves by reading a book and if they manage to read a little, a page, they say they have a headache. It's because they're not used to reading, but they call it a headache. So they like 'yarns', that's their entertainment. I tell them about Belgium, anything, what happened to me in such and such a community... and they tell me about their deeds in the war. They exaggerate a little, they laugh at themselves.

Sometimes the Europeans have asked me:

'Rogelio, don't you ever feel lonely?'

That's a very European question. Because loneliness is the great problem there. I always tell them no, my problem here is that sometimes I have wanted to be alone and I can't be, that I'm never alone, I'm always with the compas, eating, sleeping, on the march...

Sometimes I take up a book and they gather round me. There are few books at the front. The compas read the party pamphlets, the catechists read the bible and sometimes a student brings a book, but there's very little to read, it's not the custom. So I want to read and they come round me and ask me to read to them. They're curious to enter the world of books!

Ever since I've been a priest I've always prepared my sermon in writing. This has the advantage that you don't just stand up and spout any old thing. On their way past the compas see me writing:

'What are you writing Rogelio? Don't you write beautifully?'

'I'm preparing what I'm going to say to you at mass.'

'But you know already, why are you writing it all down?'

They think I don't need to prepare at all. But I always have done. When I improvise I feel uncomfortable, it doesn't come out right, because of the language but also because that's how I am.

If I start reading the missal because there's nothing else to read they come up to me:

'What are you reading, what's it about?'

And that's just an excuse to begin a chat. They love chatting.

No, in Morazán there's no privacy. I found it very hard at the beginning. One is never alone. In San Salvador I could go to my room and listen to music, meditate, prepare my sermon. No one came in without knocking and asking permission. We priests were trained to work in a private room where no one can come in.

Not here. There's no privacy even for your most intimate needs! Not even then. We have a hole for a latrine. A hole with a few bushes round it, a little way away. Sometimes you are there and not even there are you alone. We hide. At the beginning this kind of thing really distressed me. Not so much now, though.

Sometimes I feel a great need to be alone, to meditate, to evaluate my life before this God in whom I believe, who's always asking me for more commitment. To review my life. I need these moments on my own and I withdraw a little. Just a little... The compas are capable of following you anywhere.

I hardly ever ask God for anything. I ask for very little in my prayers. A bit of strength for me and the compas. For this people in all its sufferings. It's the only thing I can ask for. I think we are responsible for ourselves and that we should be capable of facing our own problems in life. God isn't going to solve them for us.

## Celibacy

Yes, I've often been asked why I haven't married. They like the subject and now they know me a bit better, they joke about it. If there's a *compañera* present they ask:

'And what about this little *compañera*, Rogelio, wouldn't you like to marry her?'

The *compañera* is in on the joke as well. For them it's no problem whether a priest marries or not. The big problem is that they cannot imagine making a commitment to celibacy and keeping it. For many of them this is something completely impossible and stupid into the bargain.

'And how do you stand it without a woman, Rogelio? Haven't you got one at all?'

And I answer jokingly too:

'You're not going to get me involved in that hassle. I've got enough problems already!'

We laugh. But sometimes we go a bit deeper. And they understand:

'If I had got married I probably wouldn't be here. Because I'd have been worried about my wife and children. I would never have taken the decision to come to Morazán. I didn't marry, so I feel free. I can stay here, I can die here and I don't have to think that I've left my wife behind in Belgium or in Mexico. There's no responsibility that I'm neglecting. Here I am and here I shall stay. I'm free.'

They understand this, because their families are a major problem for them. Children growing up in a refuge, children abroad, a wife with a bourgeois outlook, perhaps, and what kind of upbringing is she giving the children...

The war has gone on a long time and this causes many problems. It causes real emotional traumas. There's great instability, uncertainty, their wives are far away and they have women friends here at the front and what are they going to do... The war has not just lasted a year or two... They are men, they have a macho mentality, I cannot demand that they be celibate like me. How can I ask a peasant, with his macho upbringing, not to find another *compañera*? We choose celibacy but they don't. And how hard we find it! I insist that at least they should behave decently in this, and not go with one woman today and another the next. That happens sometimes, too. Moral problems, emotional problems, which are real, and affect their work, their commitment...

In the matter of sex we are all a bit weak, we are all human beings. I don't think I'm the strongest man in the world, and if I see a pretty woman... But I can control it. I think it's also a lot to do with individual temperament. I've always felt a great deal of freedom in celibacy, it doesn't cause me a lot of grief. And this freedom, this peace of mind, I feel a lot more here at the front, where so much is at risk.

They understand all this. I think that if I married some of them would be very disappointed. Even these same compas, in spite of their jokes. I feel that celibacy is a witness in the face of the exaggerated passion for sex. And because of this witness, I can make demands of them, I can talk to them about all their sexual problems, I have nothing to hide... Even if I did have, there's no chance I could hide it. You can't hide anything here.

### Ronan Rigan

During these years I've seen their army grow. The compas have more discipline, more military training, more political education, a higher level of consciousness and a terrific lot of experience. The FMLN is a peasant army. Most of them are peasants. A few of the leaders are students, but more and more membership of the high command is being extended to peasants. Those who reach the high command have an extraordinary wealth of experience. The peasants have the advantage in some things: they know the terrain and they've suffered so much that they're tireless. If it's a question of writing something or sending a message, those who have studied have the advantage. But as they're working together and they're all *compañeros*, they don't notice the differences and there's a tendency towards a tremendous equality.

97

Do you know where I notice the difference? In the jokes they make. The peasants make very simple little jokes. The students' jokes are more sophisticated. The peasants are very sensitive and some expressions offend them. When I'm walking along talking, even to the catechists, I have to take care not to offend them. You begin to realise all the weight of the past that they carry with them. They've always been rejected, they've always been despised.

The peasants are also tremendously skilled at making simple weapons. Here we have munitions workshops where they make guns and mines, and they experiment with new devices. They even mend broken weapons, adapting any old piece of some old weapon to make the repair. It's very finicky work and they do it really well.

Sometimes our intelligence service discovers some of the lying and cheating that goes on among the enemy... An army officer sends word to the command that they are in such and such a place and have fulfilled their mission. The command is satisfied and orders them to return.

But it's false, they haven't done what they claim at all. They say it because they don't want to go on, because they are scared stiff of crossing land sown with the mines our peasants make, which are really deadly.

But for the aircraft and the bombing we would already have won the war. On land the armed forces can't do much. They advance because they can count on air support, and each time they find themselves in difficulty, they call in the planes.

So there is the clear consciousness that the army depends on the aircraft, bombs and helicopters sent by the United States. Everyone is conscious that this is a war against the United States, against imperialism. This is a very common idea, even among the simplest peasants: we are confronting North American imperialism. Even the children speak about this. Sometimes we make *piñatas* for them,* and I ask:

'What are we going to call the *piñata*?'

'Ronan Rigan!' (sic)

So they can break his head! That's what everyone feels. And they know that it's because of the US that we haven't already won the war and it's because of the gringos that the war has become tougher and so cruel.

---

*Hanging pots made from a gourd or papier-mâché, painted to resemble a face or animal, and filled with sweets and small gifts. They are hung up at children's parties, then broken with a stick so that the sweets cascade out [Ed.].

In 1981 the North Americans judged that the war was more a political than a military problem. They tried to win it by genocide and they failed. In 1983 the North Americans considered that the war was fundamentally a military problem and they planned to win it by increasing the size of the army and they still failed. For the North Americans the war in 1986 has become a major political and military problem of still greater dimensions and for which they have no solution, neither genocide nor military aid...

The army has made not the slightest progress with the political side of its counter-insurgency plan. The principal reason for this failure lies in their strategic incapacity to make significant concessions to the masses. On the contrary, they have merely continued to oppress them. Their capacity for making concessions has gone no further than sporadic hand-outs of food — a discredited form of charity which fails even to relieve the hunger of a single day, and certainly cannot make the people forget 50 years of repression. These actions only confirm the profound contempt they feel for a people whom they believe to be incapable of thinking and struggling with consciousness of their own interests, but whose principles and human values are far superior to those promoted by the system in which we live...

In a country as small and densely populated as El Salvador, every square kilometre where the armed forces can no longer sustain their military power in a stable manner, where the judicial and political authority of the government cannot be maintained, and where another form of power is beginning to develop in embryonic or partial form, will be further evidence of a clear duality of political and military power between the FMLN and the army, which will seriously weaken the North American counter-insurgency plan.

In El Salvador, a country with 244 inhabitants per square kilometre, crossed by many roads, full of towns in every direction, there is no such thing as an isolated mountain or rural area. In this sense every inch of land lost constitutes a vital change in the balance of the war. At a modest estimate of the territory where the FMLN has more control or more authority than the armed forces, we could say that this extends to about 2,000 square miles, about a quarter of the country [Joaquín Villalobos, 'El estado actual de la guerra y sus perspectivas', *Estudos Centroamericanos* 449 (1986), 169-204].

## A new church

I see a new church being born. When I look at our small Christian base communities I think: perhaps something new will be born here within a few years. All over El Salvador, people are working for this, in their own localities. With confidence. There are a lot of us; we are many. There are quite a lot of priests outside the war zones working along the same lines and many other priests are setting up communities. We have learned a lot during these years of suffering. Something new is coming into being.

We are contributing to the creation of this new church, which marches alongside the people and is inspired by the gospel. Our hope is that it will become so strong and solid that the bad example of the institutional church can do no more damage. For the *compañeros*, even though they are not believers, this kind of Christianity, this kind of church is a sign. They appreciate and respect it very much. We priests and nuns have always considered ourselves to be the core of the church, at the centre of everything, but the new church that is emerging has the people as its centre. I want the church to lose all its power and become an almost invisible church. Then we will have the opportunity to speak of the gospel, to discover in the very depths of ourselves what it means to be Christians, and what the Christian message is really about.

Really the revolution is a form of spirituality. When I see compas going out on a special mission, to penetrate a key army barracks for example, to carry out an operation right under the enemy's nose, it always makes me think. They're going on this mission and they know very well that in all probability they will never come back. The comandantes address them, they shout slogans, and off they go with great dignity, pleased that they are going to do something great. They go with the mystical feeling that it is worthwhile giving their lives. They are young, and they could run away if they wanted, because they want to live, but still they go.

Yes, there's a spirituality involved — the spirituality of being part of something greater, projecting yourself towards society, offering your contribution, giving your life. Exactly what happens in a truly Christian community.

A political meeting is also a kind of service. It really is. There's applause, the word, singing, slogans, shouting. Only the bread and wine are missing, but there's always a meal of some sorts at the end.

Sometimes I think that there's no difference between Christianity, in this sense, and Marxism, experienced more as a spirituality than an analysis. We start with the person of Christ and they with this important historical project. Seen from this angle, there's not so much difference.

At any rate, just to say that a Christian is a communist, and a communist is a Christian, is oversimplifying things. We must go deeper into this relationship. Is there something which is specifically Christian? I think so, though I don't know how to describe it. Sometimes I think that while we have the chance to contribute something we contribute it. And if we cannot contribute anything then we contribute nothing! There are so many people I'd like to discuss this with, but up till now I haven't talked it over with anyone... What is it that is specifically Christian? Whatever they say, a socialist society is much closer to the gospel than a capitalist society. It's clear that Marxists can teach us a lot, especially the value of collectives, submitting your private interests to the interests of the collective project, dedication to the community, to a people. Although you find this dedication and these values in the gospel, most of us have had an upbringing which was more bourgeois than Christian and which teaches us a love which goes so far and no further, my family first, a diluted gospel which is just individualism, spiritualism...

Something in our Christian education which we can use, however, is this acute sensitivity it has given us to the value of the human person, every human person. The danger, of course, is that we become individualistic, but the opposite danger is that with the collective we forget the value of each person. Because each person is worth a great deal. He may be old: he is still of great worth. She may be a baby: she is invaluable. I remember my parents with my mentally handicapped brother, who was a wreck. I saw in their generosity my brother's true value, and his true worth in the eyes of God.

I'm not saying that we have a monopoly on individual values, personal values, but sometimes in the midst of grand projects, and the broad sweep of political lines, these things can be forgotten. At such times we have to sit down and consider what to do about them. Obviously we must all join in and take up the fight... but that old man over there? We must consider him, too. Are we to leave him out? I don't know if you follow me.

Why should I deny it? I'm really concerned that the people should have faith. It concerns me because I think that faith brings happiness. And I want the people to be happy, that's what I want, that's what concerns me most. That they should be happy in this life, and that they have another view of death. But I think we

101

priests must take care not to speak too easily about God. We are so accustomed to going on and on about God. How often we repeat that God directly intervenes in our lives...

'But Father, if he intervenes, when is this going to end? So many years of war and so many thousands dead? What is God up to?'

So I try to talk to them, not to convince them, because I can't convince anyone! And it's not so obvious that God does intervene, is it? My faith is too fragile. We talk:

'Do you believe in victory?'

'Of course we do! That's why we're here, can't you see?'

'But there are thousands and thousands who don't believe. So what you have is faith in victory. That's a kind of faith, because not everyone believes in this victory, or expects it or wants it. The United States, the most powerful country in the world, is against us. All those waverers who support Reagan are against us. Here are we, with a few weapons, a starving people, with few resources... If you make a list of all the obstacles and then we solemnly proclaim that we are going to win the war, why it's madness! Proclaiming that victory will come is pure faith.'

That makes them think. The difference is that I connect my faith in victory with my faith in God, in the God of Jesus, who guarantees this victory and who will have the last word.

When I speak about God I feel suddenly very timid. Perhaps it's because of this fragile faith I have. And if I feel timid, imagine these 'compitas' when someone says to them:

'God doesn't exist!'

The faith of these peasants is tremendous. God is there, behind the door. They connect everything with God:

'Yesterday there was an air raid and we weren't hit, thanks be to God.'

It surprises me. Because these people have suffered such a lot. Bombings, murders, massacres....

'God acts, Father.'

That is what they say it to me. They are sure of what they say.

'God is with us, Father, because if it hadn't been for God, it would have been even worse.'

They always defend God! And whatever happens, God always defends them!

You know what it means for a faith like that when someone comes and says:

'God doesn't exist!'

They come to me:

'Is it true that there is no God, Father?'

Sometimes I feel what they want from me is that I should affirm my own faith with certainty. But out of timidity or respect I can't do it, I don't like doing it. My faith is fragile, because the faith that is certainty is no longer a faith.

'Is it true that there is no God, Father?'

I am moved when they ask me this, because they are expressing confusion. They are demoralised, they feel weakened. Faith gives them a horizon, the strength not to collapse, it gives them a way of life. If a peasant's faith is not respected, if it is struck down, this destroys what was always his source of strength and life. It's a dangerous matter to try to pull up this root all in one go. That's why the compas, the leaders, respect the faith so much.

And when there is no need for strength to struggle, because the class struggle is over, will there still be faith? Some say that faith is a cultural thing and that the more advanced the people become, the more they mature, the more they will reject faith. They say that to have faith is to have an unscientific view of the world, that only marxism is scientific. Faith, they say, is only for mobilising consciousness at this stage, and that afterwards there will be a qualitative leap and that will be the end of all this religion business.

Certainly I believe that we are never going to arrive at such an ideal society that there will be no reason to hope for anything more beyond it. We will never make people so perfect that there will no longer be this enemy within, which continually lures us into individualism.

I think it will always be a source of happiness to have this God who guarantees us a full life. Our efforts to come up to the level of Jesus and of the values represented by the gospel will always be valid. I don't think these values are transitory. I don't think they are values that need to be superseded. They are real values.

Suppose we win. We are going to win. Then an even more difficult time will come: the time for reconstruction. Then will come times of temptation, decadence, mistakes, accommodation, forgetting our principles... Don't you think we will need a permanent revolution within the revolution? If so, it will always be a help to us to have a God who invites to go further. I am no one to talk, but that's how I see it. We are marching towards happiness, but there will always be more road ahead of us. We are fighting for happiness, but there will always be failings. There are human relationships with all their problems, there is ill health. There will always be questions, dissatisfaction, we will always have limitations to overcome.

Faith has made me happy, it gives me great hope, it gives me a horizon. That is why I refuse to give up believing. A peasant once said to me:

'Faith is love, Father. Without faith you can't live.'

That's why I'm so concerned that the people should have faith. So that they can live. I want this faith for all. Why not?

It is in our action that we come together here, marxists and Christians, in the same struggle for the same people. I myself feel that we are on the same road, seeking the same values. The compas have a poem, which they call 'The Party'. In it they say what it means for them to join the party. To join the revolution, I say.

Unless you've come to give
your heart and life,
don't bother to join,
because even before you have,
you start to leave.
If you've come to find
a bed to have a cushy time in,
don't bother to join,
because here a wound
is the most coveted prize.
This place is fit
only for sacrifice.
Here you must be
the last to eat,
the last to keep,
the last to sleep,
the first to die.

What could be more Christian than that?

I think our most important role is to give hope. That's my reason for being here. If they told me, Look, the circumstances are such that you cannot say mass, you cannot do pastoral work, you cannot hold discussion groups; the only thing you can do here is be with the compas, with the people, march along with them, I would still stay.

For this people who believe in God, the word of faith is a source of strength, value and hope. Having a priest with them is for them a sign that God is with them.

The same goes for me, I feel it too. When I feel wrecked and exhausted, and don't want to do anything, when I share their anguish and sometimes I don't even want to talk, and I'm even more fed up than they are, their presence gives me encouragement. They are the ones who give me hope. This is what we share and what we give one another, the hope that God is with us, that we are going to win. That's why I'll never leave. Until we win the war.